THE ONLY SKILL THAT MATTERS

THE
ONLY
SKILL THAT
MATTERS

THE PROVEN METHODOLOGY TO READ FASTER, REMEMBER MORE, AND BECOME A SUPERLEARNER

JONATHAN A. LEVI

LIONCREST
PUBLISHING

THE ONLY SKILL THAT MATTERS

The Proven Methodology to Read Faster, Remember More, and Become a SuperLearner

ISBN   978-1-5445-0436-0 *Hardcover*

978-1-5445-0434-6 *Paperback*

978-1-5445-0435-3 *Ebook*

To the 200,000+ SuperLearners out there in the world.

Thank you for giving my life purpose.

CONTENTS

SPECIAL INVITATION

Thank you so much for picking up a copy of this book. If you are passionate about improving your reading, memory, and learning, I'd like to invite you to join our thriving community of over twenty thousand members. There, you can share your progress, learn from others, and stay up to date on the latest new content. To join, please visit http://jle.vi/bonus.

INTRODUCTION

——

"Why are you trying to read that?" the principal asked.

Silent sustained reading. Eighth grade.

Of all the students, in all the classes, this evil bastard had pulled up a chair behind me.

By now, I was used to interrogations anytime something went wrong on campus, and even to the occasional teacher reminding me of my very limited potential.

But this time, even I was surprised.

I looked up from my Java 2 textbook—which I understood almost nothing of—and sheepishly replied, "I want to learn how to program computers."

What followed took every ounce of the disdain that comes from decades of reprimanding problem children in a British boarding school.

He scoffed.

If you've picked up this book, chances are you know what it feels like to wish you could learn faster.

You've spent the late hours studying, trying to keep up with your peers, your industry, or your passions.

You've faced the exam you thought would kill you, struggled to transition between industries, or even missed that big promotion.

But even if you have kept up, no matter.

You no doubt can feel the pace of information and change constantly creeping up around you, slowly drowning you as you attempt to tread water.

And deep down, you know the unspoken rule of the game we're all playing: in our information economy, if you can't learn quickly and effectively, you're going to get left behind.

In the next decade, this trend is only going to accelerate as we transition into a society of nearly 100 percent knowledge workers.

And in that time, every single knowledge worker in the world is going to have one of two conversations. In the first, your employer will thank you for your service and tell you that it's no longer needed. Your job has been outsourced, eliminated, or automated. Best of luck.

In the second conversation, they'll use phrases like "irreplaceable," "leading expert," and "invaluable asset." Then, they'll ask you what it would take to keep you around.

Which conversation do you want to have?

Fortunately, there is a better way to learn. A way that harnesses your brain's innate abilities to make learning both easy and fun. A method that makes new information as memorable as your most cherished memories. That allows you to accumulate knowledge faster than you ever thought possible. This method is based on proven neuroscientific principles and has been developed and refined for over 2,500 years. Once you know it, you'll be able to learn anything you desire, from industry trends to foreign languages, in a fraction of the time.

In this book, you are going to learn the techniques that

comprise this method in an easy, entertaining, and step-by-step way. You will learn to use the evolutionary strengths of the human brain to create and retain strong, linked memories. You'll learn to maintain those memories effectively over time. Plus, you'll learn strategies for reading faster, optimizing learning, and maintaining peak brain health.

Over the last five years, I've taught this SuperLearner methodology to over two hundred thousand students and readers in 205 countries and territories. Those students have gone on to pass every exam imaginable, from the bar exam, to technical certifications, to the MCAT. They've used these techniques to change careers, start businesses, learn languages, and master musical instruments. And while some subjects do lend themselves more to these techniques than others, we've yet to find a topic that can't be learned easier using them.

Are you ready to claim your birthright and become a SuperLearner? Keep reading.

CHAPTER 1

INFORMATION OVERLOAD AND THE EXPLOSION OF KNOWLEDGE

———

Unless you've missed the last couple decades, you know what information overload feels like.

Every year, there are six hundred thousand to a million new books published in English alone. Not to mention the millions of books published in other languages.

And that's just books. More and more, as a society, we are consuming our information from an ever-growing flood of newer media. These range from the traditional media, like magazines, television, and newspapers, to the more modern blog posts, podcasts, audiobooks, and videos. In short, we are producing (and consuming) more information than ever before.

Not long ago, books were a precious commodity. People were lucky to own one or two books, and they read those books over and over again, savoring each page. In 1731, when Benjamin Franklin established the first subscription library, he pulled all kinds of strings to amass just forty-five books.[1] Today, around 250 years later, the Library of Congress holds over thirty-nine million books. And again, let me remind you: that's just books. (Every weekday, the library receives about fifteen thousand items, adding about twelve thousand of them to the archives).

For the most part, this is a very good thing. Throughout human history, progress has been loosely correlated to how easy it is for the average person to create—and access—knowledge. In this light, we might look at a few key events throughout history as major "turning points" in our development. The foundation of our world, then, started with the invention of writing, around five thousand years ago. Sure, we take it for granted today, but writing is what allowed us to asynchronously record and deliver information and knowledge from one person to another. No longer did we have to transmit information

---

1   Walter Isaacson, *Benjamin Franklin: An American Life* (New York: Simon & Schuster, 2003), 104, Kindle.

from person to person orally. More importantly, we no longer had to rely on our imperfect memories to store that information. This might not sound like a big deal, but it is. After all, every great empire is built on technology. For the British, that technology was ships. For the Romans, it was roads and metallurgy. But thousands of years before that, it was writing and accounting that helped the Sumerians build the first massive kingdoms.

Of course, even then, new information technology was not without its critics. Socrates, a proponent of memorization and oral education, often spoke against the use of writing, claiming it "weakens the memory and softens the mind."[2] Imagine that. I guess every generation has their own version of "that thing is turning your brain to mush!"

Controversial or not, the creation of writing was a massive technological breakthrough. It empowered us to disseminate important texts—mostly religious ones, mind you—to millions and millions of people. This enabled mass education and mass collaboration on a scale never before seen in human history. Pretty great, if you stop and think about it.

In the 1440s, Gutenberg's commercial printing press took this a step further. While printing presses had existed in

2   Walter J. Ong, *Orality and Literacy* (Abingdon, UK: Routledge, 2002), 78.

Asia for hundreds of years, none of them were as practical or as scalable. Gutenberg's design, once perfected, enabled printers to easily reproduce and distribute many copies of books. This, in turn, made it much faster and easier to spread thoughts and ideas using the printed word.

For centuries after this revolutionary invention, the rate of information produced and consumed climbed steadily—and for good reason. Information—and therefore education—became cheaper and more readily available. This meant a more educated public, which, in turn, meant that more people were able to contribute to the growing body of knowledge. By the time he wrote Part III of his autobiography in 1788, Benjamin Franklin proudly proclaimed that his public library system had "made the common tradesmen and farmers as intelligent as most gentlemen from other countries."[3] In fact, Franklin himself was a perfect example of the effect a well-educated public can have on the body of human knowledge. Though he was denied a formal education and dropped out of Harvard over ideological differences, his life of autodidactic learning served him very well. In his lifetime, Franklin made significant contributions to the fields of politics, literature, science, governance, and more. And, in his roles as both postmaster for the

---

3   Benjamin Franklin, *The Autobiography of Benjamin Franklin*, (New York: PF Collier & Son Company, 1909), 66, Kindle.

US colonies and one of the most prominent printers and newspaper editors in the New World, he personally presided over this information explosion.

The next waves of innovation in information technology were, without a doubt, revolutionary. But despite that, they all had one flaw in common with traditional print publishing. Be it radio, broadcast television, or satellites, the next few waves of technology still had gatekeepers. Besides the occasional community radio or TV show, it was just about impossible for your average person to spread information on a massive scale. This meant that the information shared was, for the most part, carefully curated.

All this changed with the advent of the internet. Sure, in the early days, you needed to know a bit about computers and HTML to produce something people could actually read on the internet. But no longer. Today, technological literacy is a given, and all it takes to share information is a couple of clicks. You don't even need to be able to write intelligibly today...you can vlog!

This, once again, has resulted in an absolute explosion in the amount of information we as a society produce. I need not scare you with the statistics of how many millions of posts, tweets, videos, and podcasts are shared every day on the internet because chances are you've felt it. And sure, most of it is, for lack of a better word, noise. But a great deal of it is not.

Consider this for a moment: Of all the information you've consumed over the last week, how much of it came from "traditional" media outlets? You know, names like CNN, *The New York Times*, NPR, or Random House? Just twenty years ago, that number would have been 100 percent. But today, in the era of The Huffington Post, Medium blogs, independent podcasters, and self-made YouTube stars, it's probably less than half. In fact, of the three million podcast downloads, tens of thousands of books, and over two hundred thousand online course enrollments I've delivered over the last five years, not one of them came through "traditional" media outlets. And guess what? More and more of your favorite authors, podcasters, and bloggers are bypassing the gatekeepers and publishing their work directly to you.

So, like I said...explosion.

This doesn't just have repercussions for "casual" information like self-help books or interesting business podcasts. This democratization of knowledge creation has played out in more and more fields. At first, the explosion of information started in only the most technical of fields like science and medicine. Think about it: at the turn of the nineteenth century, a doctor was a doctor (and a veterinarian too, if the situation called for it!). But then, as the amount we knew about our bodies began to increase, it was no longer possible for one person to maintain a working knowledge of it all. Over time, the medical profession fragmented: pediatrics, internal medicine, oncology, orthopedics, radiology, psychiatry, and so on. Today, it's even more fragmented. If your child has a tummy ache that just won't go away, today, you'll likely be referred to a pediatric gastroenterologist. Need a nose job? You'll likely see a craniofacial plastic surgeon who does nothing but noses. And heaven forbid you should develop a rare form of bone cancer. You'll need to find a good musculoskeletal oncologist.

But this explosion of knowledge hasn't stopped there. Indeed, it has expanded outward. From the sciences and computer programming to history and law and even to "soft" skills like sales and marketing. Today, the floodgates are wide open, and every profession is experiencing the benefits—and the detriments!

Furthermore, because there are exponentially more of us creating this new knowledge, the pace at which we do so is not linear, but geometric.

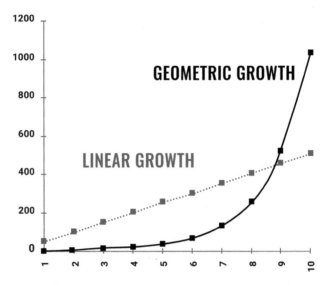

For those of you who struggled with math as much as I did, here's a helpful picture illustrating what I mean.

Just as Moore's law famously stated that computer power would double every two years (and costs would halve), knowledge grows in a similarly exponential way. Twenty years ago, computer science students at Stanford could rest easy knowing that their four years of training would prepare them for the job. Today, much of what they'll learn is obsolete even before they graduate.

It's clear why. After all, with the insane amounts of knowledge and technology at our fingertips, anyone, anywhere, can innovate. A few decades ago, the early programming frameworks like C were developed over the course of years by massive corporations like Bell Labs. Today, someone such as David Heinemeier Hansson can build a framework like Ruby on Rails (which powers many of your favorite websites) in his spare time—in about six months!

One afternoon, during the writing of this book, I broke for lunch on the rooftop patio of my office building in the bustling high-tech hub of Tel Aviv. Once there, I couldn't help but overhear a loud, heated debate between the founders of a cybersecurity startup. From the sound of it, they had discovered the perfect job candidate. She was friendly. She was ambitious. Heck, she was almost overqualified for the job. There was only one problem: she wanted to travel for six months before starting.

The conversation that ensued reads eerily like a marketing campaign for this book:

"It's a long time, but she's really talented."

"You're right. She's amazing. But six months? Our industry moves at light speed. Six months is an eternity. Even if she were Steve Jobs, in six months of traveling, her skills will be completely irrelevant!"

"You're being a little unreasonable, aren't you?"

"Am I? Did you see that article I sent you about the innovation happening in micropayments right now? In just three months, those guys have created a whole new freaking industry! And she wants six?"

Something tells me she didn't get the job.

Whereas it used to be only doctors and programmers who struggled to keep up with the pace of their field, today, it's almost everybody. Marketing managers who aren't caught up on all the latest consumer psychology research. Sales professionals who haven't learned the latest features of their software of choice. Professionals in every industry who want to take their career to the next level but are struggling to keep up with the work they already have—much less make time for "leisure" learning like foreign languages, musical instruments, new skills, or pleasure reading.

Perhaps you've already felt this overwhelm. Perhaps you're in one of the few professions that hasn't felt it—yet. One way or another, let me assure you: it's coming. And until this rapid progress brings us the technology to "download" information directly into our gray matter, the overwhelm is only getting worse.

Fortunately, there's a better way. A way to not only choose the right things to learn, but to absorb them with relative ease—and actually remember them! Fortunately, you can become a SuperLearner.

CHAPTER 2

THE ONLY SKILL THAT MATTERS

———

"The illiterate of the twenty-first century will not be those who cannot read and write, but those who cannot learn, unlearn, and relearn."

—ALVIN TOFFLER, AUTHOR OF *FUTURE SHOCK*

In modern life, there are a lot of skills that are important.

As a twenty-first century human, you need to know how to navigate social relationships, get along with technology, stay informed about politics, obey laws, balance your finances, make smart career decisions, choose a healthy diet, and about a million other little skills that help you thrive in today's world.

Of course, none of these skills actually matter if you aren't able to learn them effectively.

You may be familiar with Maslow's hierarchy of needs:

Proposed in 1943, Maslow's hierarchy teaches us that unless we meet our more basic needs, we are unable to even think about what comes next. If, for example, you aren't getting enough oxygen, you really don't care much about food and water. Until you have a safe place to sleep at night, well, you're probably not too worried if you are living up to your full potential at work.

If you think about it, learning is the same way. It's the gateway skill to unlocking every other skill you need in life. Until you develop the basic capacity to learn as a child, you aren't too worried about multiplication tables—much less philosophical questions. You're much more concerned with cracking the elusive skills of lifting your head up, crawling, and then, one glorious day, walking.

Finally, once you've developed that basic ability to learn, the next most important skill, of course, is language. After all, how are you supposed to learn things higher up the hierarchy if you can't understand the way they're communicated? This is why we each spend a year or more of our early lives learning to speak and communicate. The subsequent skills of literacy, general knowledge, analytical and critical thinking, and eventually original thinking are skills that we develop over the first twenty to twenty-five years of our lives, from kindergarten all the way up to our graduate degrees. In this light, effective learning stands out as the only skill that really matters—because once you have it, you can learn literally any other skill.

Here's the thing:

At any point in your life, did anyone, educator or otherwise, actually teach you how to learn?

Or, for that matter, how to best use the ten-pound mass of neurons and synapses you call your brain?

Think back for a moment. You had years of physical education classes teaching you the importance of exercise. There were a few health and biology classes teaching you how your individual cells and organs work. I bet there were even some very uncomfortable sex ed classes that taught you how to safely use your other parts...but what about your brain?

How is that fair?

When you buy something as simple as a refrigerator—something that was designed by a team of engineers to be as easy to use as possible—it still comes with a fifty-page user's manual! That manual gives you helpful information about every single feature plus exact instructions to follow in case you experience difficulties. And yet, when it comes to the single most complex object in the known universe (your brain), you're lucky if you get even a hint as to how to actually use it.

This is why many of us struggle through school and learning in general. We suffer excruciating boredom learning new material, waste endless time reviewing that material, and in the end, we forget it after the exam anyways. I mean, be honest: How much do you actually remember from high school trigonometry?

For me, this journey was a particularly painful one. As early as preschool, I stood out as the typical "class clown," unable to sit still or keep quiet. For my first few years of life, it was cute and endearing. Early report cards sent home by my first-grade teacher tell of my difficulty keeping up with other students. Teachers acknowledged me as a happy and friendly child and, for the most part, were willing to forgive my outbursts and distracting behavior.

By the age of eight, the novelty had worn off. One of my earliest memories of school is staying after class for a series of strange tests with my second-grade teacher, who had previously been in charge of special needs education. I didn't realize it at the time, but my parents were quietly having me tested for ADHD—and the results weren't promising. Though I was never officially diagnosed, it was pretty clear that I would struggle with this learning disability for the rest of my life. My parents considered medication but, after seeing how other children reacted to it, decided against turning their creative, happy child into a drugged zombie. I can't say I blame them.

For the rest of my elementary school years, I would be a problem in the classroom. Luckily for me, I was blessed with some very compassionate—and very patient—teachers. Though my report cards still mentioned distractibility and difficulty keeping up, and I still struggled to understand what was being taught in class, I received an incredible amount of support, which kept me from ever being held back a grade. Anyways, I was much more passionate about after-school activities and didn't much care how I was doing in school.

All this changed in sixth grade. I found myself in a new school—three times the size of my old one—and suddenly, school was a serious place. My classes were hard. Really hard. Even English, my strongest subject, was somehow over my head. Mathematics and science, on the other hand, were outright impossible.

But I wasn't just falling behind in the classroom. Whereas other kids seemed to be learning the valuable social (and romantic) skills necessary to survive middle school, I found myself in a scary, new world with new rules and norms that I didn't understand. Developmentally, I was completely unable to keep up. As my peers were developing and growing into young adults, I looked in the mirror and saw an immature and incapable kid with nothing to be proud of. In class, I was ashamed of being one of the "dumbest" kids. Outside of class, I unknowingly dressed, behaved, and expressed myself in ways that made me stand out—and not in a good way.

It wasn't long before the other kids took notice. I soon became one of a handful of students at the brunt of every joke. I was picked on, bullied, and humiliated in just about the cruelest ways you can imagine. In time, even the small group of fellow misfits I called friends turned on me, joining in on the cruel pranks and humor at my expense. Here, again, I simply couldn't understand; why was this happening to me?

By eighth grade, I was in the deepest depression imaginable. Every day, I spent my time in class scribbling helpful reminders on my arms, ranging from "Shut The F*** Up" to "I hate...me." At the age of thirteen I was already considering suicide, and had I not been an only child, I might just have gone through with it. Luckily, someone actually took note, and though she made sure to keep our friendship private for reputation purposes, she went to the school counselor.

What ensued remains one of the most painful experiences of my entire life. Watching my parents—who have always loved their only child more than life itself—struggle with the pain of having almost lost me gave me a shock to my core. With their support, I resolved to stick around for a while and lean in.

By freshman year, school became even more difficult, and so I was very fortunate when a friend introduced me to the medication his parents had given him years ago: Ritalin.

Suddenly, everything changed for me. I marched home to my parents after my first time on the drug and was eventually given a prescription of my own. Almost overnight, I went from being a C student to having nearly all As. My confidence soared. I was sharper in conversation and more able to control my rambling outbursts. Of course, Ritalin didn't make me any smarter, and I still didn't understand a lot of what was going on in class. But, with my prescription bottle in hand, I developed a new trick. Every day, I would come home at three o'clock, take my second dose of the day, and lock myself in my bedroom till it was time for bed. If I couldn't learn as easily as others seemed to in class, I would just have to work harder—and take more medication—to catch up. Subconsciously, I developed a healing mechanism that would guide the rest of my life: I vowed to never again be the kid who didn't understand.

The results of this tactic were incredible. I got fantastic grades and SAT scores. I built a multimillion-dollar internet business. I was admitted to UC Berkeley and graduated with honors. Then, I sold my business—all by my twenty-fourth birthday. Needless to say, my newfound confidence (or ego), built on the back of my accomplishments, also helped my self-esteem. Truthfully, though, even with my "trick," I'd struggled a great deal to keep up at Berkeley. In fact, I changed majors to something easier three times just to survive, eventually landing on the easiest subject I could find: sociology. And of course, like most students, I forgot what I'd learned the moment I left the exam room—but who cares, right?

It seemed that most of my problems were behind me.

Fast forward to 2011. I'm admitted to INSEAD, one of the world's top business schools, for a condensed, ten-month MBA in both Singapore and France. It was bad enough that I'd have to cram in two years' worth of material in my weakest subjects. But on top of that, I'd have to pass certification tests in two foreign languages, move countries twice, maintain a side business, and somehow still have time for all of the travel and networking that MBA programs are really about.

My old trick? Well, that just wasn't going to work. Months before the program even began, I received a 1,200-page reading list, most of which I didn't understand at all. The best part? My instructors assured me that this reading would give me a head start—for the first week of school.

What the heck had I signed up for? And to think, I had already gone off of Ritalin.

Fortunately for me, at that time I was interning at a small venture capital office in Israel. There, I met a very smart (and very unusual) man named Lev Goldentouch. In addition to speaking three languages fluently, Lev had earned his PhD in machine learning and information theory at the tender age of twenty-seven. He also was married to Anna, an educator who had spent years teaching memory and speed-reading techniques both at local universities and to children with learning disabilities. Because of all this, Lev was, without question, the fastest reader I'd ever met. Upon arriving to work at 9:00 a.m., he would read five to ten articles over his morning coffee, flooding my inbox with articles about our common interests by 9:15. What blew my mind more than anything, though, was that Lev not only comprehended information at this speed: he remembered it. A conversation with Lev was like consulting Wikipedia, only with more humor.

I had to learn how to do this.

Over the next six weeks I trained with both Lev and Anna in what I would later term "SuperLearning." When I went off to INSEAD in the fall, I was a new man. Sure, I still needed Ritalin to sit still in the classroom for eight hours. But I was now not only able to keep up with my peers; in some subjects, I was able to surpass them. On more than one occasion, other students pulled me aside to ask how I found time to read all the case studies before class, or why I had "given up" on the exam and left an hour early. They didn't understand: I had finished it.

Socially, I never found my place at INSEAD. I was one of the youngest, and least mature, members of my class. But academically, I felt truly superhuman.

After graduating, I let my new SuperLearning skills run free. First, I tackled some of the issues I'd had as a young man. I devoured books on social psychology, body language, attraction, and charisma. I built upon the knowledge that Lev and Anna had taught me, diving deep into neuroscience, memory, and learning theory. I diagnosed and fixed my own health problems by reading books on kinesiology and sports therapy. I developed myself spiritually and emotionally with a wide range of books on life's journey. I even read business books and took programming courses, attempting to launch a new software startup.

And then, I had an idea.

What if, instead of referring people to an overbooked Anna, we built an online course, where anyone could learn these skills?

I didn't know the first thing about recording videos, editing, developing learning materials, or content marketing—but I knew how to learn. One weekend, I opened forty-five or so tabs on everything from pedagogical design to branding and even how to use basic editing software. I figured out not only how to create online courses but how to create great ones. I then worked diligently to translate the materials from Hebrew to English. Two months later, on December 26, 2013, we launched the first Become a SuperLearner online course.

The rest, as they say, is history. In a short while, we were one of the top courses on the web. Within five years, we would have over two hundred thousand students, nearly a dozen online courses, an award-winning podcast, and two books. At every step of the way, I would apply my SuperLearning skills to whatever it took to grow the business, from marketing to leadership, to lighting and audio, copyrighting, and more. Today, I am blessed to say that my business is one of the leaders in the accelerated learning space. More importantly, the books I read outside of work have helped me build lasting relationships with a group of friends—and an incredible woman—who love me and support me in all that I do.

Not bad for a kid who almost didn't survive the seventh grade.

Behind it all, I credit my ability to learn as the reason I am where I am today. Learning has not only made me a happier, healthier, and wealthier person—it's saved my life.

But the SuperLearner method hasn't just changed my life. Over the last five years, I've made it my life's mission to prevent as many people as possible from ever feeling the suffering I felt: the suffering of feeling stupid, or of being unable to understand the complex world around them.

Along this journey, we have had some truly incredible stories come out of our SuperLearner programs. Stories like that of Dr. Juli La Rocca. After struggling through medical school, Juli became pregnant and gave birth during residency. Unfortunately, at that time, her relationship also became abusive, unhealthy, and dangerous. Determined to make a change, she turned to the SuperLearner program and began upgrading her ability to learn effectively. This empowered her to do her own research and create a powerful, holistic toolkit for developing emotional strength and navigating single motherhood.

What's more, it unlocked within her a deeper passion for learning. Juli picked up a copy of our Branding You program and, within a matter of months, learned everything she needed to know to launch a successful online business teaching her method to other single moms. At the time of this writing, she is leaving medicine to launch http://Unbreakable.mom. I have no doubt that she'll impact the lives of many people and create the best possible life for her and her daughter, Zulei, along the way.

Or how about the story of Dwight, an overwhelmed Air Force pilot who was battling to keep up with all the learning and memorization needed to succeed as a commercial pilot. Dwight spends as much as four hours a day commuting, leaving him almost zero time for studying. Fortunately, after trying some other accelerated learning programs, he discovered SuperLearner and immediately began reaping the benefits. He figured out an ingenious way to practice the skills while driving and was able to effectively triple his reading speed and learning capacity. Gone were the days of endlessly reviewing and forgetting, and in no time, Dwight realized that he had essentially memorized the entire manual—in a fraction of the time. He learned all of this so quickly, in fact, that in 2019, he'll be promoted to an entirely new plane. I'm confident that with the tools taught in this book, he'll ace it in no time.

> To see my full interviews with Dr. Juli La Rocca, Dwight, and many other successful SuperLearners, visit http://jle.vi/bonus.

With stories like these, it's easy to see why my team and I believe that learning is the only skill that matters. After all, if you can learn effectively, you can learn—or become—anything you want. With these skills, you can go from being a depressed social outcast to a happy and successful entrepreneur. You can go from being a struggling young professional to a leader in the company of your dreams. Most of all, you can go from wherever you are today to wherever it is you aspire to go. And that's why, now, it's your turn to learn.

CHAPTER 3

LEARN LIKE A CAVEMAN

———

I want you to imagine, for a moment, that you're a Paleolithic caveman or -woman, roaming through the savannah, about a hundred thousand years ago. It's a sunny, pleasant morning, and though you're a little bit hungry, you're not famished.

As an average Paleolithic human, you are, of course, highly intelligent. In fact, you don't know it, but you are literally the most intelligent species ever to have walked this earth. You can remember and find your way back to the tribe, the watering hole, or the secret locations of your winter food supply just by observing your surroundings, the sun, and the stars.

If you're a female, your expertise is most likely foraging.

You can identify thousands of plants, their nutritional or medicinal uses, when they grow, and where to find them in a pinch. If you're a male, you are likely a skilled hunter. You regularly track and predict the migrations of all types of beasts, collaborate and coordinate kills, and prepare carcasses to prevent rotting. You can skillfully craft an arrowhead in seconds, create a fire in minutes, and construct a shelter in hours.

Beyond these very useful survival skills, you also have a vast understanding of social systems and ties. You are versed in the language, religion, and culture of your tribe. In fact, you know the history and genealogy of everyone in it. This knowledge extends outside your tribe as well. You can easily identify neighboring tribes by their markings and dress. You know which tribes roam which areas, which ones are hostile, and which ones are valued trading partners. All of these skills, in time, will help your descendants conquer the entire planet—for better or for worse.

What you don't know is how to read or write.

In fact, you've never even seen a written character, aside from the occasional cave painting.

Does this bother you?

Not in the least.

You see, the types of information that gave our Paleolithic ancestors a survival advantage didn't come from textbooks or Bible verses. It was olfactory, gustatory, and visual information—in other words, smell, taste, and sight.

Allow me to explain: smell and taste, which are connected senses in the brain, were among the first to develop. In fact, they predate even the mammalian brain and are hardwired into the much older, deeper, reptilian brain. This is why, when someone passes out, smelling salts will wake them up even when sound or touch fail to do so. It's also why smell and taste are by far the most memorable of senses. Don't believe me? Head on over to the department store, and see if you can find the cologne or perfume that your first love used to wear. As you smell it, you'll be instantly taken back decades to the thought of them—whether you like it or not! And yes, the same goes for Mom's home cooking.

If you think about it, this makes perfect sense. If you're a dinosaur roaming Pangaea two hundred million years ago, you'd best remember what rancid meat or poisonous plants smell and taste like. If you don't, it's only a matter of time until repeatedly gorging on them kills you. Plus, chances are, that's going to happen before you have the opportunity to mate. You know what that means: your anosmic (unable to smell) genes aren't getting passed forward. Evolution: 1, You: 0.

Behind smell and taste, the next most survival-inducing sense is, of course, sight. Sure, hearing is great, but as you might have noticed on *National Geographic*, predators rarely give a friendly shout-out before attacking. That's why, whether you're a saber-toothed tiger or an early hominid, you aren't going to get very far unless you can remember what danger looks like. You need to see (and remember) when the river is too high to cross, when the shape of the snake means "venomous," and the subtle difference between the leaf that heals you and the leaf the kills you. Ultimately, this is the type of information that has helped us, and millions of other sighted species, survive over the last five hundred million years.

Closely related to our sense of sight is the ability to locate ourselves. After all, our sense of location is wholly based on being able to recognize and remember our visual surroundings. Make no mistake: for just about every land-faring species, this skill is life or death. Forget your way to the watering hole? Lose track of that winter food supply? Bad news, my friend. Evolution wins again.

The point is, after hundreds of millions of years of cruel evolution, you, me, and most of our mammalian friends are left with brains that are really good at remembering smells, tastes, and sights. As *Homo sapiens*, we're especially adapted to learning in ways that are vivid, visual, and experiential. Scientists refer to this as "the picture superiority effect." And though many of you have been led to believe that you're an "auditory" or "tactile" learner, the truth is, we are each naturally gifted at remembering pictures. What we're not so naturally gifted at is learning from boring lectures or dense textbooks. Heck, we only invented writing systems some five thousand years ago, and the average person couldn't read until a few hundred years ago. Evolution is an all-powerful mistress, but she's not a fast-moving one.

Knowing this, I'd like you to think back to your days as a student. Even if you were lucky enough to study something very visual, like medicine or engineering, what percentage of your learning would you call vivid, visual, or experiential? What percentage came via boring textbooks and rambling lectures? Think, for that matter, about the most recent thing you attempted to learn—even if it was outside of school. How did you approach it?

The most innovative schools, from the established Montessori to the new-age MUSE, know this and have modeled themselves accordingly. Students in these schools don't learn geometry from a textbook; they learn it by building real structures and observing real phenomena. They don't study biology by listening to a teacher drone on; they learn it by cultivating gardens that feed the entire school.

Fortunately, it is not too late for you to claim your birthright as a SuperLearner. You just need to return to the basics. To learn like a caveman. But first, let's examine what it actually takes for your brain to learn something.

CHAPTER 4

THE ADULT BRAIN AND HOW IT LEARNS

———

"Knowledge is to be acquired only by a corresponding experience. How can we know what we are told merely?"

—HENRY DAVID THOREAU

By the time I entered fifth grade, my mother had realized that she had a knack for supporting children with difficulty learning. For this reason, she decided to supplement her psychology degree with a teaching certification. Through months of diligent study, she gained a much deeper understanding of the things she had long known from intuition and her experience as the president of my developmental preschool. One idea she mentioned to me in passing, after a long day of certification classes, has always stuck with me:

"If it's not in the hands, it's not in the head."

Now that we understand how our brains evolved to learn, this should come as no surprise. This idea stuck with me, though, for two reasons. First, hearing it out loud it helped me understand why I'd struggled in the classroom up until that point. But second, and perhaps more importantly, it was the moment I realized that some ways of learning were better than others. At ten years old, this was the first time I was exposed to the idea that there were conditions to learning.

As it turns out, having something "in the hands" (or, in other words, experience) is only one of the requirements of adult learning.

Fast forward fifteen years, to 2011, and I have just completed Anna and Lev's intensive tutoring. My mind has been blown by the realization that by simply changing the way I approach learning, I can learn literally anything—with ease. For the next year or so, I'm like a human sponge. I set about absorbing everything I can get my hands on, from health hacks to more advanced memory techniques to speed-reading research, and more. As Anna, Lev, and I began creating our first online course, I continued devouring not just "hacks" and "techniques," but also the foundations of learning itself. I wanted to understand: How do we learn, actually?

As you can imagine, there is a lot of research on the subject, and quite frankly, I'm not going to bore you with even a fraction of it. While I'm a firm believer that you need to understand how something works to use it confidently, there's also such a thing as a "minimal effective dose." After all, you don't need to understand the exact gearing ratios of a manual gearbox to drive a stick shift.

In my research, I happened upon one researcher whose work stood out in particular: Dr. Malcolm Knowles. Educated at Harvard and Chicago University, Knowles began his career at the National Youth Administration and later became the director of adult education at the Boston YMCA. After World War II, Knowles earned his PhD while serving as the director of the Adult Education Association. For the next fourteen years, he served as an associate professor of adult education at Boston University. There, he authored over 230 articles and eighteen books, nearly all of them on what he called andragogy: the science of adult learning.

In short, this was a man who deeply understood how adults learn.

Dr. Knowles's work stands out not because it used cutting-edge neuroscience or because it revolutionized our education system. It did neither. What stood out about Knowles's work was his singular focus on understanding the needs of the adult learner. Never before had so much thought gone into not just the motivations behind adult learning but the actual requirements to make it happen.

So, what are these requirements?

FOUNDATION

First and foremost, Knowles understood that as adult learners, we have a lot more life experience than children do. Not only do we have a larger body of knowledge to draw from; we've been around the block a few times, made our fair share of mistakes, and had our fair share of wins. For this reason, as adult learners, we come into the learning environment with some strongly held beliefs about the way things work. To the untrained learner, this prior experience and knowledge can be both an asset and a liability. On the one hand, it is easier for us to understand the world around us—and, as you'll see later on, to create powerful connections between our memories. On the other hand, holding on to our beliefs makes us less open to new information—even when it's correct.

What does this mean for us as adult learners? Put simply, it means that we should actively leverage our prior knowledge and experience when learning. We must compare and contrast the things that we're learning to the information that we already know. How is it different? How is it the same? How can the information and experience we already have contribute to our understanding of this new and exciting topic? Far too often, we approach a "new" subject as if it's completely foreign, when in fact, the whole of human knowledge is connected in some way. By making this powerful mindset shift alone, you will almost instantly become a more effective learner. (Especially when combined with the memory techniques you'll soon learn).

NEED TO KNOW

We're all familiar with the age-old questions asked by generation after generation of bored students: "Why do I need to learn this? When am I ever going to use _____?" You've probably asked it, and you've almost certainly heard it.

Have you ever noticed, though, that it's almost never young children who ask these questions? As Knowles understood, something changes in the way that we learn as we mature. By the time our brains reach adulthood, we become much more discerning. We are no longer willing—or able—to sit down and memorize information because "teacher says so." Suddenly, as we reach puberty, we want to know: Why? Why is this information relevant to our lives? And no, some lofty, philosophical answer is not enough. Have you ever tried to tell a teenager to do their algebra homework because it will make them a "more well-rounded person"? The reply is generally some variant of "No, thanks." Instead, as our brains mature, the "why" that we seek is more practical—more functional. We not only want to know why this information is valuable; we want to know how we're actually going to use it and whether or not it will help us reach our goals!

Once again, this is a simple mindset shift, but one that produces noticeable results. By simply considering the ways in which you will apply a piece of information, you increase your ability both to focus on and to remember it. Later on in this book, when we learn the powerful skill of pre-reading, we will leverage this exact principle to great effect.

> For your convenience, I've provided a ready-made worksheet to help you identify your goals and your "why" as you go through this book. To download it and other exclusive bonuses, visit http://jle.vi/bonus.

READINESS

Adult learners want to know how they're going to apply the information that they're expected to learn. Unfortunately, even that is not enough for our highly discerning brains. In fact, in addition to knowing how we are going to use that information, we want to know that it's going to happen soon. Again: try telling a flippant teenager that learning history will be useful when they have children of their own. Good luck! Most adult brains don't want to learn something unless they have a pressing and immediate need to. This was true in Malcolm Knowles's day, and it's even more so in today's era of information overload and endless busyness.

Luckily for us, most of the things you'll learn as an adult are things you need to know now, for work or some practical application. With that said, it's still important to consider the logical consequence of this principle. Adults learn best through active practice and participation. Design your learning experience accordingly! After all, there's no better way to convince your brain that this stuff is immediately useful than by, you know, immediately using it! This is why piano lessons rarely start with boring music theory, and why the best computer programming courses start by building something useful. There's hardly a "pressing need" for another useless "hello world" application.

ORIENTATION

Because adult learning is so much more pragmatic and practical, it's logical that it should be centered around problem-solving. Adolescents tend to learn skills sequentially as they build up their body of knowledge. In adults, however, Knowles found that it's best to start with a problem and work towards a solution. If you think about it, this makes perfect sense. As adults, we want to know that the things we're learning are immediately useful. What better way to do this than to solve actual problems or challenges? This way, practical application is "baked in" to the learning experience.

For this reason, as we go about our own learning, it's important to pay attention to the orientation of problems versus solutions. When in doubt, it's always best to look at our learning through the lens of problems and solutions. Manipulating the information and considering realistic applications is necessary for effective learning. In fact, research shows that it leads to longer lasting and more detailed understandings of the things we learn.[4]

SELF-CONCEPT

Alongside the importance of prior experience and practical application, adult learners have yet another requirement: we need to be involved. Have you ever sat back and passively watched a video or course on YouTube, only to forget everything you learned? Or read a book where the author told you everything you needed to know, but somehow, it's still not enough?

---

4   John Clement, "Students' Preconceptions in Introductory Mechanics," *American Journal of Physics* 50, no. 1 (1982): 66, https://doi.org/10.1119/1.12989.

As adult learners, Dr. Knowles argued, we have much more established identities. In addition to trusting our own experience, we trust our own judgment. And why shouldn't we? After all, we've been living with ourselves for decades! Who knows us better than we know ourselves? For this reason, when we come to the table as learners, we want to be involved in the planning and evaluation of our education. We want to make decisions based on our own situations, compare our experience with that of others, choose our own adventure, and get our hands dirty.

This is why, even in our structured online courses, we give students plenty of choices along their journey. They can choose to dig into the supplemental resources on any given topic or limit themselves to the required course materials. They can choose to go at the pace we recommend, or, with our full support, slow things down. They can share their experiences in the course forum and see what paths others are taking. Furthermore, we encourage students to skip certain lectures if they don't have a pressing need for a specific application. In doing this, we empower the learner to feel like an equal partner in their learning experience. We do away with the hierarchy of "experts" and "students" and instead compel them to take ownership over their learning from day one. We know that simply giving learners this responsibility has a massive effect on their enjoyment and their success.

The next time you find yourself stuck in a rigid learning environment, such as a normal online course or a highly structured corporate training, take a step back and think. How can you customize your path, make decisions, and reclaim some ownership over your experience? Later on in the book, when we discuss the concept of "brute force learning," you'll discover a great way to do just that.

MOTIVATION

Finally, let's talk about the most dreaded subject of all when it comes to learning: motivation. As we've mentioned before, adult learners are rarely able to muster the energy simply because someone else tells them to. It's not until the stakes are real, like a big promotion on the line, a degree we've dreamt of, or a skill we need to keep pace with our peers, that we're really able to learn.

Why is this?

Well, in addition to being highly discerning and practical, adult learners respond better to internal motivation. The external motivation of someone telling you that you "should" do something might be enough to get you to see a movie or try out a new restaurant. But it won't be enough to get you to commit your precious time and energy to learning something new. In short: you can't expect educators, employers, or even friends to motivate you to learn something. Instead, the drive to learn must come from within you—from the principles of learning we've already established. If you want to build up the motivation to learn something, dive deep into your why. Why do you want to learn it? How will you use it? Why will your life be better once you have? Do this simple focusing exercise before and during your most challenging periods of learning. You'll find that it's a useful way to motivate yourself, even when no amount of coffee will.

* * *

Now that we've been introduced to Knowles's six principles of adult learning, I'd like you to think back to a time when you truly struggled to learn something. For me, this was freshman year algebra. In your case, how many of these principles were being leveraged effectively? Chances are, the answer is one—or fewer. Besides leveraging your prior knowledge of other types of math, I bet your algebra teacher rarely connected what you were learning to your prior experience in the real world. It's also safe to say that you had no pressing need or practical use for figuring out the values of X and Y. So much for internal motivation. I'm sure you had plenty of opportunity to learn in a problem-centered fashion. You did it night after night! But I'm guessing that nobody invited you to help create the lesson plan.

This is the unfortunate but true reality of most educational environments today. What works for us as learners individually rarely works for the group as a whole. In a traditional classroom, it's impossible for even the best teacher to check off every requirement for every student. Imagine how much time it would take to ask each student about their prior experiences or how they plan to use the information. Even worse, imagine the chaos of allowing each of them to customize their own unique curriculum. It simply doesn't scale. And like it or not, our current educational system was designed for the mass production of good little worker bees. Anything that doesn't scale, doesn't fly.

Fortunately, you, reading this book, have a choice. Now that you know the rules, you can create your own conditions. You can learn the way your brain wants to learn. And it all starts with a little preparation...

CHAPTER 5

AN OUNCE OF PREPARATION

———

A woodsman was once asked,
"What would you do if you had just six minutes to chop down
a tree?"

He answered,
"I would spend the first four minutes sharpening my ax."

—UNKNOWN

Oftentimes, when we sit down to learn, we are full of excitement, passion, and enthusiasm. We are eager to dive in, to sink our teeth into this new subject, and give it our best shot. But the truth is that while it's great to have enthusiasm for learning, enthusiasm without planning can do more harm than good.

A few years ago, I decided that I was going to learn my fourth language—Russian. I was passionate about it. Second, as an up-and-coming accelerated learning expert, I wanted to demonstrate the power of what I was teaching by learning a relatively "difficult" language. Third, I already speak a Germanic, a Latin, and a Semitic language, so I wanted to try something really different. Finally, I knew how important it was to fulfill the "pressing need" and "immediate use" criteria. While there aren't very many native Mandarin speakers in Israel, I'd have no shortage of Russian speakers.

With the näive goal of learning Russian by the end of the year, I dove in with a fury. I memorized both alphabets (cursive and block) and their pronunciations in a few days. I memorized hundreds and hundreds of new vocabulary words in a few weeks. I began studying the grammar and forming basic sentences. I even learned to touch type in Russian. I was on fire.

A few months later, I landed in Moscow, eager to flaunt my new skills to my Russian friends.

I was in for a rude awakening.

On the train from Domodedovo Airport to the city center, I noticed an advertisement for Citibank. As it turns out, Citibank's slogan in Russia at the time was a very friendly one:

"Citibank. Always with you. Always for you."

Except in Russian, it was written like this:

"Ситибанк. Всегда с Вами. Всегда для Вас."

Wait, what?

I understood most of the words—and even their choice to use the collective, formal version of "you." This was a concept I knew from my prior knowledge of the Spanish word, *usted*.

But why were they using two different words for the word "you"?

Oh, crap.

As it turns out, in all my study of Russian, I had neglected to understand one crucial element:

There are about six ways to say every word (and pronoun) in Russian—depending on the context.

But that's not all. I quickly learned that my vocabulary list—which I thought was sorted by importance—was clearly not. Whereas I knew such useful words as трубка (tube) and мешок (sack), I did not know the difference between вход (entrance) and выход (exit). As you can imagine, the security guards at the Kremlin were less than amused.

What had gone wrong?

Poor planning.

Instead of sitting down to get a broad overview of the Russian language—a view of the forest from thirty thousand feet—I had gone straight for the trees. In all of my excitement, I neglected to develop a plan for balancing between vocabulary and grammar. I never stopped to look at the "big picture" and understand how the case system actually works. I simply jumped in at what looked like the beginning. And to this day, I am a below-average Russian speaker because of it.

The idea of preparing and structuring your learning in a logical way beforehand comes up a lot in accelerated learning circles. In his accelerated learning book disguised as a cookbook, *The 4-Hour Chef*, Tim Ferriss shares his framework for preparing to learn anything faster. It goes like this:

> Deconstruction: How small can I break things down into their basic units of learning, such as individual vocabulary words or grammatical rules?

Selection: What are the 20 percent of those units that will give me 80 percent of the benefits (Pareto's Principle)?

Sequencing: What is the best order in which to learn these units?

Stakes: How can I use psychology or social pressure to condense my timelines and push myself to learn faster?

With this process (and the other techniques in the coming pages), Ferriss has become an accomplished author, a successful investor, a top podcaster, a skilled chef, a champion sumo wrestler, and a record-holding tango dancer.

Whatever you're learning, thinking ahead is key.

Recently, I interviewed Zach Evans, creator of the popular Piano SuperHuman online course. During the interview, Zach explained to me that most of the results he generates for his students come from simply thinking ahead. Through years of teaching, he has developed a system for breaking things down into individual skills or sections and then tackling them in the right order. Zach also pointed out that unless we plan out our learning in a methodical and deliberate way, we fall prey to bad habits, wasted time, or complacency. Zach himself learned this one day by accidentally leaving his camera recording during a practice session. When he reviewed the footage, he discovered that he'd wasted the entire two hours playing pieces he already knew.

For the full interview with Zach Evans and other exclusive bonuses, visit http://jle.vi/bonus.

Before you begin to study a new subject, there are a handful of questions that you must ask yourself. These questions will do more than help you determine the most efficient way to learn something, though. In fact, when you learn the almost annoyingly effective memory techniques later on in the book, you'll see that learning something the wrong way can have permanent consequences down the line.

Here are some questions I encourage you to spend time considering before diving into any learning project.

- **Why am I learning this** information, and how and when will I actually use it? You probably noticed that this first question immediately checks off a few of Dr. Knowles's requirements. But beyond that, it also helps us determine just what we're going to focus on in the first place. Chances are, you're not learning Russian to communicate with construction workers, right? In that case, learning words like трубка (tube) is probably not worth your time. If, however, you're learning Russian to travel in the former USSR, then you should probably prioritize basic grammar. (Heads up: I also suggest learning practical words like "exit" and "entrance.")

- **What level of understanding or knowledge do you need?** One question that I've long felt is missing from the preparation conversation is that of depth. After all, there are many levels of understanding and knowledge. The ability to remember a list of facts is very different from the ability to think originally on the subject. So ask yourself: To what level do you need to know the information you are learning? Do you need to be able to recite other people's works word-for-word and challenge them for your PhD thesis? Or, do you simply need to know where to look something up the next time a patient presents those symptoms? The depth to which you need to know something dramatically changes the way you should approach learning it—and how much time you'll spend on it!

- **How can this information be broken down into small parts? How can it then be recombined into broader categories or themes?** In this question, we "break it down." What are the units of information in this new subject? Are they verses of a poem? Functions in a programming language? Chords on an instrument? Or words in a lexicon? Once you've determined these individual units, how will you classify them into groups, such as historical periods, key signatures, or parts of speech?

- **What are the most important things to learn based on my personal goals?** As you likely know, Pareto's Principle states that 80 percent of the benefits come from 20 percent of the work. This means that unless you're looking to become the world's best in a given subject, you can usually save yourself 80 percent of the effort in learning. In music, for example, most of us can skip learning the individual frequencies of each note. In English, it's safe to say that most non-native speakers shouldn't bother with the future perfect continuous case. In fact, from years of living abroad, I can attest that they should avoid the confusion altogether!

- **What is the right order in which to learn this information?** Learning a heap of grammatical rules doesn't make a lot of sense if you don't know enough words to form a single sentence. Similarly, it's not very useful to learn to read music until you know which keys play which notes. As I learned when I tackled Russian, the order in which you learn things really matters. Remember: you can never reclaim time spent learning the wrong things.

- **How will I actually access this information?** Knowing how you'll access the information you're learning is often just as important as knowing which information to learn. When I began studying Russian, I made the mistake of organizing my memory palace (a powerful tool you'll soon learn) alphabetically. At the time, this seemed as logical a way to do it as any. But how often do you write a sentence and think to yourself, "What I really need is a word that starts with a K?" More likely, you're searching for a specific part of speech like a noun or an adverb. It wasn't until I interviewed star SuperLearner student and polyglot David Sanz Stinson that I realized my mistake. By then, it was too late! Don't make this mistake yourself as you prepare to memorize new information. If you're studying for the bar exam, ask yourself: Do you need to access laws by their order in the penal code? I'd assume not. You need to know what type of law they pertain to. Memorizing in this way is a very different—and much more useful—project.

· **What will your study schedule look like, and how can you compress timelines?** As Tim Ferriss teaches in his books, Parkinson's Law states that work expands to fill the time you allow it. We all know the feeling of writing an entire semester's final paper in a matter of days—or hours. So why not use this nifty psychological hack to our advantage? By structuring out our study sessions methodically, based on the questions above, we ensure consistency and persistence. Plus, by adding high stakes, social pressure, and condensed timelines to the mix, we kick ourselves into high gear. My friend Benjamin Hardy, psychologist and author of the book *Willpower Doesn't*

Work, calls these planned constraints "forcing functions." Want to learn AcroYoga fast? Prepay for an advanced workshop three months from now. Hoping to learn a new technology at work? Volunteer to teach a workshop on it next quarter. By adding real-world stakes, you'll be motivated to create an ambitious study plan—and actually stick to it.

- **How will I measure and track my progress?** To keep track of whether or not you're moving forward at the right pace, it's important to have a clear metric of success. For this reason, I often teach students about the concept of "S.M.A.R.T." goals. The most effective goals are: Specific, Measurable, Ambitious, Realistic, and Time-based. Why is this better than any other goal, you ask? Well, if your goal is to "get better at Excel," it's pretty hard to assess that. You're likely to drop off or put in very little effort. If your goal is to "learn six new features of Excel, including pivot tables and macros, by December 31," that's a different story. With this S.M.A.R.T. goal, it becomes much easier to monitor yourself and course correct along the way. Plus, remember that what gets measured gets improved, but what gets measured and reported improves exponentially.

- **What will I do if things don't go to plan?** With any luck, the previous questions will challenge you to tackle some aggressive and ambitious learning goals. In a perfect world, you would achieve all of them, in record time, every time. But the higher you shoot, the more likelihood there is of failure—and we all slip up sometimes. No matter how positive you are, nothing is more frustrating than watching your best-laid plans fall apart. In these times, it's easy to spiral downward, beat yourself up, or give up altogether. That's why the best managers plan for occasional failures ahead of time. What exactly will you do if you fall off the bandwagon or get stuck on a particular subject? How will you get back on track and prevent one little slip up from derailing you and causing you to give up completely—a phenomenon psychologists lovingly call the "what-the-hell effect." Will you book extra sessions with a private tutor? Make up the time on the weekend? Adjust your study schedule and give yourself some slack? If you have a specific plan ready for when you inevitably fall off track, you'll minimize the damage and ensure that you waste as little time as possible.

For your convenience, I've transformed these questions into a ready-made learning preparation worksheet. I suggest printing it out and using it every time you start a new learning project. To download it and other exclusive bonuses, visit http://jle. vi/bonus.

Armed with these nine questions, you are well prepared to...well...prepare. You now understand why thinking ahead and creating a methodical success plan is far from a waste of time. In fact, it's quite possible that every minute of preparation will save you an hour or more of deliberation. That's why, from now on, every time you set out to cut down a learning tree, I know you'll take a good hard look at the forest first. Then, make sure your ax is razor sharp.

CHAPTER 6

WHY (AND HOW) TO 10X YOUR MEMORY

—

Years ago, I had the great honor to interview Harry Lorayne, widely considered the godfather of modern memory improvement. In fact, *TIME* magazine once called him "the Yoda of Memory." What a nickname, right?

Since 1957, Harry was on the vanguard of rediscovering the ancient, lost art of superhuman memory. Throughout his illustrious career, he wrote over forty books and publications on the topics of memory and magic. He also founded his own memory school, coached individuals and major corporations, and spent decades in the public spotlight. Harry is perhaps best known for his dozens of appearances on *The Ed Sullivan Show* and *The Tonight Show* with Johnny Carson, where he regularly memorized and recited the names of up to 1,500 audience members—in order.

Why, then, have you never heard his name?

When I asked Harry why, in his sixty years of teaching these techniques, he was unable to bring them into traditional schools, his answer was this:

"I made a big mistake...I started to interview the teachers first...and they all insisted: 'We don't use memory.'"

Lorayne shared a story of walking into a classroom, pointing to a poster of the periodic table, and asking a "silly" question.

"I've been out of school for a very long time. I noticed that you have the periodic table on the wall here. Do you still teach that?"

"Of course," replied the teacher.

"If you teach it, do you still test it?" Lorayne continued.

"Absolutely," replied the teacher.

"Then could you tell me: What mental calisthenics would a student have to use in order to fill in the blank?"

This continued for a good ten minutes, before the teacher sheepishly admitted:

"I guess they would have to remember it."

And therein, my friends, lies the problem.

As Lorayne wrote in one of his early books, "There is no learning without memory." The problem is, memory has a bad rap. Even if they don't always show it in the best of ways, educators today know what you now know—that learning must be experiential. It must be engaging. And it must draw upon the learner's own experience and knowledge. Thus, in an effort to do away with rote memorization, educators and policymakers have thrown the baby out with the bathwater. Except where unavoidable, they've done away with anything that even resembles memorization. But in doing so, they've completely neglected the foundational—and highly experiential—skill of memory mastery.

Don't get me wrong: for the majority of things you need to learn, rote memorization doesn't work. But that doesn't mean that all memorization is bad. Quite the contrary. As Lorayne painstakingly pointed out to educators decades ago, you can't "know" something unless it's securely stored in your memory.

This is even more important if we wish to upgrade our

overall learning prowess. I mean, what's the point of increasing our learning speed, if we're just going to forget everything we learn shortly thereafter?

For my full interview with Harry Lorayne and other exclusive bonuses, visit http://jle.vi/bonus.

Most of you have probably heard the quote from Woody Allen: "I took a speed-reading course and read *War and Peace* in twenty minutes. It involves Russia."

Indeed, with your average speed-reading course, that's about the level of comprehension you can expect.

If you want to read and remember faster, doesn't it make sense that you upgrade your memory first?

In our SuperLearner courses, I like to illustrate this with the metaphor of a garden hose, a funnel, and a bucket.

Imagine that the hose is your reading speed—or your listening speed, if you're a fan of audiobooks. When everything is working normally, the hose feeds information into the funnel, which represents your working and short-term memory. This, in turn, moves information into the bucket—your long-term memory.

Imagine, now, that you switch out the garden hose for a fire hose. Suddenly, instead of a calm stream of water, the overflow immediately blows your funnel to smithereens. A fraction of a second later, your bucket overflows as well.

This, more than anything else, is the problem with your average two-day speed-reading seminar. Without upgrading the infrastructure of your memory, you're destined to fail. Until you understand how to input information to your working and short-term memory in a way that makes it stick, you won't remember much of anything in the long term. Furthermore, in order to organize and store all the information you input, a simple bucket isn't going to cut it. No, to be able to learn and memorize everything you aspire to, you're going to need a swimming pool—and a way of maintaining that swimming pool.

Of course, even with the memory techniques you're about to learn, no swimming pool can avoid some evaporation and water loss. You see, even with advanced memory techniques, your brain will naturally forget "unused" information to keep things running smoothly. After all, though your brain has a theoretical capacity of 2.2 petabytes, it's also a bit of an energy hog—at least relative to the rest of your body.

At just 2 percent of your body mass, your brain consumes

around 20 percent of your body's oxygen and energy.[5] For this reason, you have two dedicated centers deep inside the brain—the hippocampi. Their primary job is to figure out what is worth keeping and to get rid of everything else. Thanks to the hippocampi, our brains are incredibly adept at forgetting. And while it may be a source of frustration when you're looking for your keys, it's also part of the reason the human brain is so insanely efficient.

Your brain runs on about twenty watts of power—a little less than two of those eco-friendly CFL light bulbs. According to Stanford researcher Kwabena Boahen, a robot with similar processing power would consume at least ten megawatts.[6] That's ten million watts—or about as much as a small hydroelectric plant. It's unfathomable, and yet, it's true. Your brain has an insane amount of processing power, and it's five hundred thousand times more efficient than the best microprocessors ever built. How exactly this is possible remains one of the great mysteries of the universe. But suffice it to say that forgetting useless information is a big part of it. Luckily, as you're learning, there are ways to "trick" the hippocampi into storing more memories—and maintaining them long term.

---

5   Daniel Drubach, *The Brain Explained* (New Jersey: Prentice-Hall, 2000), 161.

6   Jeremy Hsu, "How Much Power Does The Human Brain Require To Operate?" *Popular Science*, November 7, 2009, https://www.popsci.com/technology/article/2009-11/neuron-computer-chips-could-overcome-power-limitations-digital.

All this sounds great—but you might be asking yourself, "Can I actually do this? I've always had a below-average memory." Nonsense. The fact is, unless you were dropped on your head or have a rare neurological disorder, there's no such thing as a "below-average memory." Over the last five years, I've interviewed quite a few national and world memory champions. These include four-time USA memory champion Nelson Dellis, Swedish memory champion Mattias Ribbing, world champion Mark Channon, and others. Guess what? Not a single one of them had an "above-average memory" when they began training. In fact, one memory games competitor, Joshua Foer, went from skeptical observer to world champion in just one year of training. Then, he documented his entire journey in the bestselling book, *Moonwalking with Einstein*. Best of all? Foer's 2006 record, memorizing a deck of cards in eighty-five seconds, wasn't even in the top six hundred by the end of 2018. (China's Zou Lujian Igm completed the feat in just 13.96 seconds in 2017.) The sport of competitive memory continues to push the limits of the human brain, but in the end, it all comes down to knowing—and improving upon—the following techniques.

For my full interviews with many of the world's top memory champions, visit http://jle.vi/bonus.

But surely, the folks who succeed with these techniques have some type of genetic advantage. After all, the only reason that Michael Phelps has won so many gold medals is his freakishly long arms. It must be the same with competitive memory, right?

Nope. In fact, a 2017 study by Radboud University sought to determine just that. For forty days, participants with average memory skills and no prior training spent thirty minutes a day practicing mnemonic techniques. At the end of the study, participants had, on average, doubled their memory capacity. What's more, they were able to reproduce these results four months later—with no further training. Just to be sure, researchers compared the brains of five memory champions to "average" people using functional magnetic resonance imaging. In doing so, they expected to see notable differences in brain anatomy, similar to the differences between an athlete's body and a nonathlete's. What they found, however, really surprised them. The hardware was exactly the same. The memory athletes were just using their brains differently.

So, how do you actually do it?

First things first, we need to master our visual memory.

As we learned from observing our Paleolithic ancestors, we are each gifted with visual memory. Perhaps, up until this point, you've believed you're an auditory learner. This is understandable. After all, through years of rote memorization and listening to teachers lecture at us, most of us have our natural aptitude towards visual memory beaten out of us by the time we reach high school. Perhaps you have always wished you had a "photographic" memory. Good news: you do! You just haven't switched it on yet. But once you do, you will see: creating mental pictures is not only much more memorable, it's also much faster. In fact, research has found that our brains are able to recognize an image in as little as thirteen milliseconds. That's 0.013 seconds! When working with students, I often compare the mental "upgrade" to switching out the engine in your car from gasoline to electric. It's an entirely different means of getting around, and so it may take some serious getting used to. But in the end, it's faster, more reliable, and much more efficient.

For this reason, a growing body of research has proven that visual memory is vastly superior to rote memorization—or any other type of mnemonic device you may have used in the past. They don't call it "the picture superiority effect" for nothing. This is also why, in one way or another, every single one of the world's top memory champions and record holders use the techniques I'm about to show you.

Now that you understand how powerful visualization is, you're ready to learn the big secret.

Are you ready?

If you want to improve your memory tenfold, create novel visualizations, called "markers," for everything you wish to remember.

Yes, you read that right.

The crux of the "big secret" behind tripling your memory boils down to imagining pictures in your head.

Anticlimactic, I know.

But that really is half the battle—or more.

At first, this might be difficult. Coming up with these markers is a creative endeavor, and many of us haven't trained our creativity muscles for years. Fortunately, we know from the research that creativity is NOT something you have or you don't. It's something you train, and something you can relearn very quickly. By simply practicing visualization over time, you will come up with more and more creative visualizations—and it'll become both faster and easier to do so.

So, what kinds of these "markers" should you come up with?

Well, as you can imagine, not all visualizations are created equal.

As a general rule, the markers you come up with should abide by the following rules.

CREATE HIGHLY DETAILED VISUALIZATIONS

First, picture as much detail as possible. By creating a high level of detail, you ensure that you are adequately visualizing a vivid, memorable image in your mind's eye. Fuzzy, nonspecific images are much easier to forget. Plus, remember that the average person's working memory can only retain three to five individual items at once. This means that breaking information down into "chunks" of three to five items makes it inherently easier to remember. That's why phone numbers and credit card numbers are formatted the way they are. As you'll see in the upcoming examples, every detail that we insert into our markers can represent a new piece of information. In this way, we effectively "chunk" more information in there, condensing it into one easy-to-remember visualization instead of three to five. This might seem a bit silly, but it's actually quite a powerful hack. At the highest level of memory competition, the difference between winning and losing comes down to how many cards or numbers the competitor can chunk into one visual marker. Every year, competitors engineer newer, more complex ways to fit more detail into fewer markers for this very reason.

OPT FOR THE "OUT THERE"

Next, wherever possible, your visualizations should include absurd, bizarre, violent, or sexual imagery. Though it might make you blush, the truth is, our brains crave the novel. Our hippocampi are very attuned to picking up and remembering things that seem strange to us. This is the so-called "bizarreness effect," and it's the reason why you'll want to keep these visualizations to yourself. When it comes to mnemonics, the stranger, the better.

LEVERAGE YOUR EXISTING KNOWLEDGE

The next important principle in developing our visual markers comes from our dear old friend Dr. Knowles. Wherever possible, you should make use of images, ideas, or memories you already have. Research has determined that our brains pay special attention to information that's related to stuff we already know and care about. This is the basic idea behind Hebb's Law, which is often summarized as "neurons that fire together, wire together." By creating connections between new information and your own knowledge, you leverage existing neural networks of people, places, and things. This creates stronger, more densely-linked synaptic connections and "tricks" your hippocampi into thinking something is more important than it is.

CONNECT IT BACK

Finally, it's important that as you create visualizations, you also create logical connections to what you're trying to remember. Obviously, a visual marker is no good if you can't remember what it stands for. For this reason, it's important to choose markers that will clearly symbolize the information you're trying to remember! As you'll see in the following examples, each visualization you come up with should explain some element of what it is you're trying to learn or remember.

* * *

With the theory out of the way, let's dive in and see the method in practice.

Let's imagine, first, that we were trying to memorize someone's name. After all, names and faces are one of the most common challenges that students come to us with, and for good reason. We all know the embarrassment of forgetting someone's name.

Let's say that we meet someone named Mike. For the sake of visualization, let's say it's Mike Tyson, and that somehow, you've never heard of him before. As soon as you go to shake Mike's painfully strong hand, I want you to take a split second, and create a marker. In this marker, picture him holding a microphone, singing embarrassingly off-key karaoke on stage.

Get it? Mike?

Now you try it.

Seriously—stop and do it, right now.

Close your eyes if you must—but don't read on until you have a visualization so clear that you can see Mike belting out the missed notes: face tattoo, lisp, and all.

By the way, when I say "clear," I must be clear myself. Visualization doesn't mean I am hallucinating the image before me, or that I see it instead of what my eyes are seeing. Things you see with your "mind's eye" are always going to be less vivid than the things you see with your own eyes. That's perfectly normal. If you can imagine a marker well enough to be able to describe or reproduce it, you're doing it right.

Got it? Congratulations! You just made your first marker.

Let's try it again. Imagine that after having your hand crushed by Mike Tyson, the next person you meet is named Alice. We can remember her name by picturing her chasing a rabbit down a hole, like Alice in Wonderland, blue dress and all. Your marker for Alice might look something like this:

Both of these visualizations work well because they are vivid, bizarre, and built out of existing knowledge and pictures in our mind. Another way to achieve this is by using people we already know as pre-existing knowledge. Imagine picturing a new person named Jenna fighting it out to the death with a Jenna we know from childhood. It sounds too simple to be true, but trust me: when you use visualizations this way, memorizing names becomes easy.

What else does this work for, you might ask? A better question would be to ask: What doesn't it work for? The answer? Almost nothing.

Foreign language words are a constant source of frustration for most learners. Where do you begin? How do you remember things that are completely new and foreign to your ear? And most challenging of all, how do you turn something so auditory—like a word in a foreign language—into a visual marker? Simple: break it down until you can find visualizations. For example: instead of trying to memorize the word *caber*, or "to fit" in Spanish, we can come up with a visualization of a taxi cab trying to fit a bear inside.

This is an example of a truly perfect marker. First, it has the sounds: "cab" and "bear," which allows us to work our way back to the sound of the word. Second, it's ridiculous! If you saw a bear hanging out of the window of a taxi cab, you'd remember it—wouldn't you? Finally, what's so clever about this marker is that it has the meaning, "to fit," baked right in. This is what I mean when I talk about using details to add additional information to our markers.

In some cases, it might be trickier to find exact matches for the syllables in a foreign language word. Take, for example, the Russian word for "thank you," спасибо, pronounced "spaseebah." Unless you decide to mix and match with the Hebrew word אב ("ba"), you'll have to get a little creative. Imagine yourself sitting in a Chinese restaurant just on the edge of Red Square in Moscow. Saint Peter's Basilica is towering over you in the background. Now, imagine that a waiter is handing you a spicy bun, steaming and covered with tantalizing red peppers. Then, to your surprise, he announces that this appetizer is on the house. To show your gratitude, what would you say? Спасибо! Spicy bun. It's not perfect, but it's highly memorable.

A fun aside: the beauty of learning foreign language vocabulary this way is that the more languages you know, the easier it gets. Someone who only speaks English wouldn't have an exact visualization for the syllable "bah." They would have to come up with an approximation like we did above. But someone who speaks Arabic, Mandarin, Hebrew, or Japanese would have no problem. Conveniently, "bah" is itself a word in each of those languages!

But what about numbers? After all, how can you create a visualization for something like a phone number? With the right system, it's easy. All you need to do is spend an hour or so learning something called the Major Method for converting each digit into an individual consonant.

NUMERAL	SOUNDS (IPA)	COMMONLY ASSOCIATED LETTERS
0	/s/, /z/	s, soft, c, z, x (in xylophone)
1	/t/, /d/, (/θ/, /ð/)	t, d, th, (in thing and this)
2	/n/	n
3	/m/	m
4	/r/	r, l, (in colonel)
5	/l/	l
6	/tʃ/, /dʒ/, /ʃ/, /ʒ/	ch (in cheese and chef), j, soft g, sh, c (in cello and special), cz (in Czech), s (in tissue and vision), sc (in fascist), sch (in schwa and eschew), t (in ration and equation), tsch (in putsch), z (in seizure)
7	/k/, /g/	k, hard c, q, ch (in loch), hard g
8	/f/, /v/	f, ph (in phone), v, gh (in laugh)
9	/p/, /b/	p, b, gh (in hiccough)
Unassigned	/h/, /j/, /w/, vowel sounds	h, y, w, a, e, i, o, u, silent letters, c (in packet and chutzpah), d (in judge), j (in Hallelujah and jalapeno), ll (in tortilla), the first p in sapphire, t (in match), one of the doubled letters in most contexts
(2, 27 or 7)	/ŋ/	ng, n before k, hard c, q, hard g or x

Once you know that system, you can create words out of the numbers and use visualizations to memorize those words with ease. Using the Major Method, for example, the phone number 740-927-1415 transforms into Crazy Pink Turtle. Even if you're new at this, that's really easy to visualize, and therefore, easy to remember.

You might not believe it yet, but it's possible to create visualizations like this for literally anything you can imagine. You can create visualizations for each card in a deck of cards, and memorize their order. You can memorize music theory or the order of chords in songs. You can memorize the geography of a region—or its entire history, complete with dates and names. You can even memorize scientific formulas by creating these types of creative visual markers. The possibilities are limitless—all you need is some practice and a vivid imagination.

But here's the thing. This technique only works if you actually use it, so starting today, I want you to use it for anything and everything you want to remember. From now on, this is just how you remember stuff—even if it's slow going at first. When you meet someone new, create a marker. When you get a new credit card, memorize it with a marker. When you learn an interesting fact in a blog post, stop for a moment, and create a marker. From now on, I want you to make it second nature to visualize everything that's important to you.

And let me remind you: there are no excuses. This technique is scientifically proven to work for everybody—young and old. All you have to do is practice—and confidently use your imagination.

Once you do, this simple technique alone—the technique of visualizing everything you want to remember—will take you very far. In fact, in that same interview conducted with Harry Lorayne, he admitted to me that he used this technique—and nothing else—throughout his career. Imagine that: memorizing 1,500 people's names, with perfect recall, on live TV.

It's remarkable. It's unbelievable. It's downright superhuman.

But it's nothing compared to what you can do with the tool you're about to learn: the tool I like to call "the mnemonic nuclear option."

CHAPTER 7

THE MNEMONIC NUCLEAR OPTION

———

For the following exercise, I need you to sit in a comfortable position, relax, and take a deep breath. This is going to seem a bit bizarre, but I need you to keep an open mind and trust me.

First, I'd like you to imagine that you're standing in the doorway to your childhood bedroom, looking in. If you moved around in the middle of your childhood, then choose the most nostalgic one. Perhaps you haven't been in that room in a few years. Maybe you haven't been back to that room in a few decades. No matter. In your mind's eye, I'd like you to travel back in time, and picture yourself standing right there in the doorway.

Next, I want you to turn to the right, and walk to the first corner of the room. If you grew up in a castle turret or a lighthouse, you can picture any other square room you're familiar with. What is in that first corner? Is it a desk? A closet? Or perhaps it's your bed. Whatever it is, right on that piece of furniture, I want you to picture two seahorses. These aren't just two regular seahorses, though. As you picture them, they're shamelessly engaged in an elaborate and messy mating ritual. It's a scene straight out of *National Geographic*. Gross! Now, I want you to get rid of those perverted seahorses by imagining them getting sucked up by a vacuum hose.

Right now, you might be scratching your head. Have faith, and do it anyways. Using your newly converted, "all electric" memory, actually visualize this happening. Right there, on your childhood furniture.

Do you see it?

Great. Good luck getting that image out of your head.

Now, traveling counterclockwise along the perimeter of the room, let's take a trip to the next corner. I want you to imagine that in this second corner, there's a delicious container of chunky peanut butter, tantalizing you. If there's a desk in the corner, you can imagine the container on the desk. If there isn't, imagine that someone has smeared the chunky peanut butter up against the walls in the corner. Yuck!

Up next, move over to the third corner, where I want you to visualize a big, messy, tangled, ball of wires. You know, the kind of ball of wires you have in that one drawer somewhere in your house? In this corner, you're going to picture that bundle of wires...and use some detail. Picture that old phone charger cable you have from the 1990s and those broken iPhone cables you still haven't thrown away. Get specific. I want you to imagine that the wires are strung all along the corner or furniture like Christmas lights. For example, if it's a closet, imagine that the wires are tangling up all of your clothes hangers, making one BIG mess.

Still with me?

All right, let's go on to the fourth corner of your bedroom...

In this one, I want you to imagine that there's a picture hanging right next to the corner. But it's not just any picture. It's your favorite historical picture of all time. You know the one. It's that picture you saw in history class and thought, "Wow...I wish I'd been there to see it!" For me, it's a famous picture of the American athletes protesting at the 1968 Olympics. For you, it might be the tanks in Tiananmen Square or the iconic photo of Marilyn Monroe. Any picture will work. Now, I want you to imagine that picture hung right there, in the fourth corner of your bedroom.

Can you see it?

By now, unless you grew up in a very fancy, postmodern-looking house, you're back at the exit to your bedroom. Once there, there's just one more visualization I want you to create. In the doorway, as you're exiting, I want you to imagine a massive "location" pin. It looks just like the kind you see on Google Maps—and it's blocking your exit. Get vivid: imagine that this pin is so big that you have to squeeze under it to escape the room.

Do you have each of those visualizations in your mind's eye? Let's review:

In corner one, you have two X-rated seahorses getting vacuumed up.

In corner two, you have a bunch of chunky peanut butter.

In corner three, you have a mess of tangled cables.

In corner four, you have a famous historical picture.

And, back at the doorway, a big "location" pin blocking your exit.

If you have all those visualizations, then once again, congratulations are in order! This time, you've created your first memory palace—and memorized the key fundamentals of why it works too.

* * *

At its core, the memory palace technique, or method of loci, is a powerful system for memorizing massive amounts of information quickly and easily. Discovered over 2,500 years ago by Simonides of Ceos, it stands out in a few very distinct ways.

Unlike other techniques, the memory palace allows users to not only memorize large amounts of information, but to do so in perfect order. In fact, once you begin using memory palaces, you won't believe how easy it is to recite information both forward and backward. This, among other reasons, is why every single memory competitor and record holder uses some variation of the technique. Best of all, it works for anyone and everyone. Study after study has shown how this simple technique can transform average people into memory superhumans. Memory palaces are so powerful, some historians believe they were used to pass along the works of Homer and other Greek philosophers. Even St. Augustine himself wrote about the technique in Book X of his *Confessions*. (Alas, the Catholic Church, which shunned the idea of obscene visualizations, was less of a fan. They burned Giordano Bruno, an outspoken proponent of the technique, at the stake in 1600. This, some suggest, may have contributed to the method's disappearance from popular use.)

In short, in the world of memory improvement, the memory palace is the undisputed champion. Of course, it's not appropriate for everything. Would I use a memory palace to memorize a handful of names or the key points of a book? Probably not. That would be like scaring off a bully with a hydrogen bomb. It'll definitely do the job, but you probably shouldn't get carried away. For this reason, I often refer to the memory palace as "the mnemonic nuclear option." There simply is no other technique that can even come close, whether in speed, ease of use, or reliability.

How can any one method be so powerful, you ask? A happy coincidence of neuroscience. You see, when used properly, the memory palace technique checks off nearly every criterion of memorability.

First, the memory palace encourages us to create novel, bizarre visualizations. These visualizations "trick" the hippocampi into remembering otherwise unimportant or unrelated information. Think back for a moment to your very own memory palace. Remember those two seahorses and their very inappropriate mating ritual? They represent your brain's two hippocampi, named after the Greek word for "seahorse" (Ἱππόκαμπος) because of its peculiar seahorse shape. And the vacuum? That's there to remind you of the hippocampus' role: to clean out information your brain deems unrelated, unimportant, or irrelevant.

Second, the memory palace helps us "chunk" information into manageable units. Sure, we can add additional detail to each location, such as the multiple seahorses and the vacuum. But when used properly, this technique ensures that we are breaking information down into groups of one to four individual units. Any more would be confusing to remember in a single location. To remind you of this "chunking" effect—and how it makes memories much stickier—I asked you to visualize chunky peanut butter smeared onto your walls.

Third, the memory palace takes advantage of something we've already learned about: Hebb's Law. As we create memory palaces, we associate new information with existing, deeply held memories: the layout of locations we know. This creates strong connections between existing memories and new ones, dramatically increasing their memorability. That tangle of messy, old wires in the third corner? You guessed it—those are your neurons and synapses wiring together. The more tangled and intertwined the new and the old become, the harder it is to take it all apart, and the harder it is to forget.

Fourth, the memory palace keeps us honest. While you may occasionally forget to create novel visual markers for everything you want to remember, with a memory palace, there's no other way. To create your palace, you must imagine each visualization in enough detail to see it in the right spot. This, of course, leverages the picture superiority effect. It's also why I had you hang a famous historical picture—pre-existing knowledge—in the fourth corner of your bedroom.

Finally, the memory palace leverages yet another one of our brain's deeply embedded evolutionary skills: spatial memory. As we learned in Chapter 3, our Paleolithic ancestors survived thanks to their ability to navigate their environment. This is why, unbeknownst to you, your brain automatically remembers the layout of your surroundings. It doesn't matter if it's a house you've lived in for years, a hotel room you've stayed in for days, or a store you step into for a few minutes. While you might struggle to remember names, numbers, or other important information every day, your brain is constantly creating strong, lasting memories of everywhere you've ever been. It knows every apartment you've ever lived in, every office you've ever worked in, and even many places you've briefly passed through.

The result?

You have hundreds, even thousands, of memory palaces inside your head, lying dormant and unused.

Even if you try, you can't help but memorize these new locations. In a 2017 study conducted on mice, researchers found that when we enter a new place with novel sensory stimuli, a small region of the brainstem known as the locus coeruleus is activated in response.[7] This, in turn, triggers a flood of dopamine into the CA3 region of the hippocampus, causing it to store a memory of the location and its details. Researchers now believe that this influx of dopamine boosts the CA3 region's ability to strengthen the synapses and form a memory of the new location. Perhaps most interestingly of all, researchers found that this response was not triggered for other types of memories. Instead, it actually appears to be specific to the memorization of new environments. In other words, research has finally figured out why the memory palace works so well. It all boils down to neurochemical changes that

7   Akiko Wagatsuma et al., "Locus Coeruleus Input to Hippocampal CA3 Drives Single-Trial Learning of a Novel Context," *Proceedings of the National Academy of Sciences of the United States of America* January 9, 2018 115 (2) E310-E316: https://doi.org/10.1073/pnas.1714082115.

occur when we activate the parts of our brains concerned with location. In 2014, another study from Dartmouth and the University of North Carolina focused on a little-studied part of the brain called the retrosplenial cortex. Their goal was to test out an even bolder hypothesis. They now believe that our memories may actually be inextricably linked to location in our brains.

This makes perfect sense. Think back to any memorable event in your life, such as the JFK assassination or the 9/11 attacks. The question we ask one another is never "What news station were you watching," but rather "Where were you when you heard?"

Location is an immensely powerful anchoring point for creating new memories. This is precisely why I asked you to block the exit to your own memory palace with a large location pin. That marker, safely stored in the doorway, represents your brain's ability to remember locations without even trying.

And now, it's time to learn how to make use of those locations.

To build a memory palace, you first need a few things. Most important, of course, is a suitable location. In reality, any location will do: past homes, office buildings, even stores you've casually strolled through. With that said,

I encourage you to remember what we learned in our chapter on preparation. Start by carefully thinking ahead and determining what information you need to know, in what order, and how you need to access it. This step alone can save you the hassle of memorizing something in the wrong way—and being stuck with it indefinitely. Ironically, the biggest "side effect" of the memory palace technique is how obnoxiously effective it is. If you memorize a speech, only to change the order of the points later on, you're likely to deliver it as memorized—for better or worse.

When, for example, I memorized my TEDx talk using a memory palace, I spent a few minutes thinking about how to logically lay it out. How many paragraphs were there? Where were the transition points? This is something you can do "in your head," by walking around the space physically, or even by drawing a quick floor plan on a piece of paper.

This type of preparation beforehand helped me determine what size memory palace I would use. It also helped me create a logical template. I chose to assign each paragraph or key idea to a specific room and memorize the important "transitions" in the walkways between rooms. When I needed to memorize the circle of fifths, a concept in music theory, I was careful to choose a square room for my memory palace. This made it easier to divide the room into twelve "stations," like the hands of a clock, with a clear understanding of which side of the room was twelve and which side was six.

As you create your memory palace, ask yourself: Will you need to access the information in a specific order? This is particularly important for things like a speech, a sequence of fifty random digits, or the chronological order of the US presidents. If so, take a moment to create a linear journey along the perimeter of each room of the memory palace. This can be done clockwise or counterclockwise, as long as your path never crosses itself. This avoids confusion or getting "lost" when the pressure is on.

In other cases, you may need to access the information by some other grouping. This might be area of expertise (names and bios), parts of speech (vocabulary), or parts of the body (anatomy). In those situations, it's best to create these logical groupings in advance. One trick I like to use is to leverage the existing logic of the location itself. I might memorize the anatomy of the reproductive system in the bedroom, the upper gastrointestinal tract in the kitchen, the lower gastrointestinal tract in the bathroom, and the brain in the office. This helps create more synaptic connections and makes it easy to find the information you're looking for.

As you lay the foundation of your memory palace, keep

in mind: there's no wrong way to create this arbitrary logic, and it only need make sense to you. In my Russian grammar memory palace, the "accusative" case is in the kitchen. I remember this logical connection by imagining two roommates accusing one another of food theft. Silly, yes, but highly effective.

Once you have the logic and layout of your memory palace, the rest is easy. Using your new, "electric" memory, create novel, illustrative visual markers for everything you want to remember. Then, place those unique markers in designated locations. Need to memorize George Washington, John Adams, and Thomas Jefferson in order? Visualize a washing machine, Adam and Eve, and the characters from *The Jeffersons*—if you're old enough to remember them. Remember: there's no such thing as a "stupid" marker, and the best marker is the one that works for you.

When choosing locations for these markers, it's best if you "anchor" your visualizations to specific areas. This could mean the corners of a room, specific pieces of furniture, drawers, or even windows. If needed, you can create very dense memory palaces by using every anchor available. If you do, though, avoid placing multiple markers in the same exact location, such as on the same shelf or pinned up to the same wall. It's far better to expand your memory palaces outwards than to overstuff them.

Another useful trick I've developed is to actually incorporate the anchor into the visualization. This serves as another connection to the new memory and makes it less likely that you'll get your locations mixed up. Instead of imagining a knife simply laying on the couch cushion, for example, I imagine it stabbing into the couch cushion and sticking out of it. Instead of imagining a washing machine sitting on the window sill, I imagine it shaking violently and breaking the window. Doing so helps me remember that the washing machine could only be near the window—and adds a bit of violence and absurdity, while we're at it.

It might sound overly simple, but that really is all there is to it.[8] Create a visualization, place it in a location, be amazed. Try it out for yourself. You'll see what I mean.

---

8   Though, at the highest levels, competitive mnemonists have developed complex ways to condense more information into their memory palaces. These typically entail a system to convert six to seven cards or numbers into just one compound visualization. But at the foundation, the technique remains the same.

CHAPTER 8

NEVER FORGET AGAIN

———

In late 1878, a little-known German psychologist named Hermann Ebbinghaus set out to prove a wild and unfounded theory. Unlike his contemporaries, Ebbinghaus believed that higher mental processes, like memory, could be studied using scientific experimentation. Over the next seven years, he developed and refined a set of experiments, which he set about performing on himself and others.

Today, we would probably consider these experiments a form of psychological torture.

You see, Ebbinghaus knew, as you now do, that any prior knowledge would give an unfair advantage and skew his results. For this reason, he developed a list of 2,300 nonsense syllables, such as "daw," "ked," and "za." Ebbinghaus would then memorize a random set of syllables by reading them aloud and attempting to recall them later on. As if this doesn't sound mind-numbing enough, you should know that just one session of this experiment included fifteen thousand recitations.

By 1885, Ebbinghaus had made some groundbreaking discoveries in the fields of memory and learning. His first book, *Über das Gedächtnis: Untersuchungen zur Experimentellen Psychologie* (translated as *Memory: A Contribution to Experimental Psychology*), was a monumental success. Besides earning him a professorship at the University of Berlin, *Memory* sparked a renaissance in the psychological and scientific communities. Before Ebbinghaus's work, little if any research was conducted on the science of memory. In 1894, however, shortly after the translation of Ebbinghaus's research, thirty-two papers on the science of memory were published in the United States alone.

To this day, Ebbinghaus's work has left lasting contributions to our understanding of memory. Most notably, Ebbinghaus discovered that our memory is subject to exponential loss. No, I'm not talking about you losing your keys exponentially more often as you age. Exponential loss means that there's a sharp, nonlinear decline in memory immediately after learning something.

This probably doesn't surprise you a whole lot. But here's the more interesting (and useful) part. Ebbinghaus discovered that with repeated, spaced repetition, his memory of the random syllables became better and better. While it would take him only a day or so to forget a set of syllables the first time around, by the second time, he could hang on to it for twice as long. By the fourth or fifth time, it would stay in his memory for weeks. Eventually, his knowledge of this information would seem almost permanent.

Graphed visually, this gradually improving memory loss looks like this:

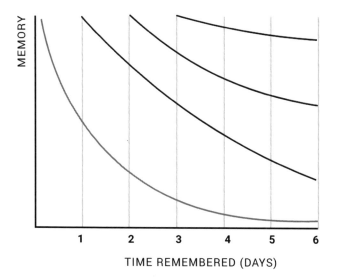

THE FORGETTING CURVE

MEMORY

TIME REMEMBERED (DAYS)

1 2 3 4 5 6

Ebbinghaus called this the forgetting curve—and it's the basis for one of the most important fundamentals in accelerated learning: spaced repetition.

* * *

In the last couple of chapters, you've learned the world's most powerful ways to make things memorable. With these techniques, you will be able to remember things faster, with greater ease, and for longer durations. You'll have a much easier time moving things from your short-term memory to your long-term memory.

But even with the world's most proven mnemonic devices, they won't stay there forever.

After all, you are fighting against millions upon millions of years of evolution.

Remember those two seahorses getting sucked into the vacuum? Every night, as you sleep peacefully, your hippocampi are hard at work, trying to figure out where they can "trim the fat" and get rid of unused memories. I'm sure they appreciate all the hard work you've done to keep things interesting for them, but ultimately, they have a job to do.

You see, in addition to all of the psychological effects

we've learned so far, our brains are subject to quite a few more. The most important of these might be the spacing effect. It states that things become infinitely more memorable if we repeatedly encounter them. You should also meet its supportive cousin, the lag effect. It states that the spacing effect is compounded when encounters are spaced out for extended periods of time. What I'm trying to say is this: learning something once, no matter how well you do it, just isn't enough. In his early work, Ebbinghaus found that there were tremendous benefits to continued review—even if he believed he "knew" the material. He called this technique overlearning, and it's an essential part of creating memories that stick.

Fortunately, there's a smart way to do this—a way that minimizes wasted time and cuts things down to the minimum effective dose. The fact is, most review is incredibly wasteful. Think back to your grade school days and those flashcards or summary sheet you undoubtedly made for that one big exam. Do you remember that feeling of working your way through that review and knowing the vast majority of the material? Sure, once in a while, you would get stuck on something you knew was challenging for you. But the rest of your study time? I think you get where I'm going.

Since Ebbinghaus's day, people have concocted a few clever solutions to this little conundrum. One such solution is the Leitner box, a system of organizing your flashcards into five separate boxes. As you study, you move your cards between the boxes depending on how well you understand the information. As you reorganize the cards, you review each box more or less frequently, based on how hard each box is.

CORRECTLY ANSWERED CARDS

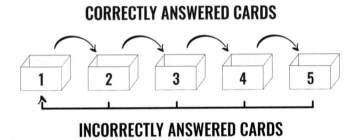

INCORRECTLY ANSWERED CARDS

This system works quite well, but it requires some serious discipline and organizational skills. What's more, it's far from portable. All it takes is a cat jumping on the table to completely ruin everything!

This is why, in the modern era, software developers have taken this concept and digitized it. Today, there are a range of spaced repetition systems (SRS) out there. These include the completely free Anki, the former memory champion Ed Cooke's Memrise, and even new upstarts, such as Brainscape.

The idea behind digital SRSs is quite simple. Create

flashcards—or download someone else's—complete with audio, video, pictures, and text. Then, start reviewing. For each piece of information, tell the software how difficult it was to answer, on a scale of one to four. The algorithm then considers your answers and reaction times and predicts when you're likely to forget that card. If you answer "easy" within a few seconds, you're unlikely to see that flashcard again for weeks—or months! If you struggle before admitting defeat, the flashcard will come up again during that study session. In fact, you'll see it again and again, until it's easy. Then, it will come up again tomorrow, and the day after that, until you can consistently answer quickly and confidently.

The end result is a whittling down of the amount of review necessary to learn large amounts of information. This allows you to either save time, if the amount of information you need to learn is fixed, or to pile on new information sooner. When I was learning what I thought was basic Russian vocabulary, I was able to learn up to thirty or forty new words in just a few minutes a day using Anki. This is because I wasn't wasting any time reviewing words I knew well. By the way, because you'll forget just about anything on a long enough time scale, SRSs help by providing even the most occasional reminder. In my Russian vocabulary deck, I have words that require review once every year or two. Just that simple review is enough to ensure I never forget them.

If you want to learn a subject fast, SRSs are a veritable secret weapon. Using apps like Anki, my students have passed the bar exam, become doctors, learned seven languages, and much, much more.

It really makes a huge difference.

Now, before I set you off to download Anki or the like, let me warn you. These software systems are developed by people who geek out on both memory and software development. The end result is that many of these apps have a sort of Jekyll and Hyde vibe. They seem simple enough when you use the web app, but download the desktop app, and you'll soon discover a sea of options, tags, menus, preferences, and databases. It is seriously overwhelming and immediately puts off many would-be users.

My suggestion is to keep it simple. Create individual decks for the things you want to learn, such as human anatomy, Norwegian vocabulary, or the chords on the piano. Avoid spending too much time customizing the format or getting fancy with different templates. Also, if you decide to take advantage of the free, open-source decks that others have shared, be careful. Whatever you do, ensure that the cards are sorted, accurate, and that they import correctly. The last thing you want to do is learn words like трубка if you don't have to.

But what about things you learn from books? Most of us read books to gain a general knowledge and perspective of new ideas, not to memorize the individual facts, figures, and quotes. For this reason, it doesn't really make sense to import each of your highlights into a spaced repetition system. Chances are, you don't care to memorize them like you would vocabulary words. Nonetheless, you do need to perform some kind of spaced repetition or overlearning if you don't want to forget everything you've read.

To make this easier, there is a range of options, depending on what your goals are. For years, I've been a big advocate of reading on the Kindle, for one simple reason: Amazon allows you to log on to their website and download or export your highlights. From there, you can put them into a document on your computer or into a cloud-based solution like Evernote. You could even set a reminder to periodically notify you to review these notes. (Yes, the Kindle app does have its own flashcard software built in, but in my opinion, it's rudimentary and not user-friendly). What's more, you could even take your highlights, write out the key ideas you want to remember from a book, and load that into Anki. Its algorithm would then determine how frequently you need to be reminded of those points.

Let's be honest, though: How often are you actually going to do that? I don't know about you, but I'm usually too excited about the next book to go back and review the last twenty I read.

More recently, however, a member of our team discovered a phenomenal app that takes care of all that. It's called Readwise, and the premise is very simple. Connect Readwise to all of your highlights (Kindle, Apple Books, Instapaper), and tell it about all of the printed books you've read. It will then create a database, adding to it the common highlights from books you've read in print or via audiobook, and send you a daily or weekly email of these highlights. What I love about Readwise is that it determines how frequently to send me highlights and then takes the burden of review off of me. All I need to do is read one email per week (or per day), and I'm performing spaced repetition on all of the books I've ever read. I like Readwise so much I've actually negotiated a two-month free trial for my readers. You can claim it by visiting www.readwise.io/superlearner.

One final note on spaced repetition. At the beginning of this chapter, I explained that visual mnemonics are not enough without spaced repetition. Well, it turns out, the converse is also true. As you dive into the world of spaced repetition and optimize your review, don't forget everything you've learned thus far. Always create visual markers—even if you don't add pictures to your flashcards. Where appropriate, remember to place those markers into a memory palace. This will supercharge your spaced repetition and save you even more review time. Some students even choose to add a custom "location" field to their flashcards. This is likely unnecessary, but it certainly keeps you honest. One great example of combining these techniques comes from my friend Gabriel Wyner, author of *Fluent Forever*. In the book, he teaches his meticulous method for combining memorable photos with spaced repetition software. With this method, Gabriel was able to learn four languages—simultaneously. Gabriel is now developing his own SRS, Fluent, which helps people learn languages in this way.

When you combine spaced repetition with the mnemonic techniques you've already learned, anything is possible. Plus, it takes a lot less time.

CHAPTER 9

PRIMING YOUR BRAIN FOR LEARNING

———

At various points throughout my university career, I struggled. A lot. Sure, I still had my "trick" of taking tons of prescription stimulants and powering through classwork, but at some point, it just wasn't enough. Back in high school, I could still somehow find the time to catch up with my classmates. In college, the workload was just too much (to be fair, I was also running a $2 million-a-year business on the side). This, ultimately, is why I changed majors three times during my time at UC Berkeley.

At two separate points, in both my freshman and junior years, I reached out to upperclassmen for help. How were they keeping up with the immense amounts of reading and remembering it all? There had to be a way to do it, or the professors wouldn't be assigning this much reading to begin with.

In both instances, the "tricks" they shared left something to be desired. They seemed far too simple to actually work, and so I brushed them off as nonsense. I had no idea that they were actually among the most effective and proven strategies for improving reading comprehension and focus.

* * *

We all know the frustrating feeling of staring blankly at a page, unable to focus, knowing that we are simply wasting our time. Or how about realizing, after spacing out for entire paragraphs or pages, that you have absolutely no idea what you just read?

This frustrating waste of time is not only normal, it's a very common problem for even the most experienced readers.

This issue, of course, is one of focus, attention, and motivation. In a perfect world, we would only read things that we have a burning, intense desire to read. We would be so enthralled by every word that it would feel like eating salted popcorn. The reality, however, is very different. The simple fact is that a great deal of the reading we do, whether for school or for work, is simply not that interesting to us. And even if it is, the sheer amount we must do stretches the limits of our attention span.

Not to worry. There is a simple solution to this phenomenon. One that will "trick" your brain into paying attention to anything you read—no matter how boring or dry. Best of all, it doesn't involve some experimental pill or potion, and it takes minutes to learn.

SQ3R

Before we dig into this skill, we first need to understand an important framework known as SQ3R. At first, this may sound like some sort of robot that spends its time hanging out with Luke Skywalker. But in fact, it's a system developed by educational philosopher Francis P. Robinson in his 1945 book, *Effective Study*. Though you may have never heard of it, the truth is, SQ3R is actually used and taught in many US schools and universities. That's probably why it was taught to me by two separate people during my university days. And about the funny name, it's an acronym for:

Survey
Question
Read
Recall
Review

SQ3R is different from the way you likely read today because it breaks the process of "reading" down into a handful of distinct steps. In doing so, it primes your brain for the knowledge it's about to receive in a few different and ingenious ways.

During the Survey step, we quickly skim or scan the content before we read it to prepare our minds for new information. If you're a trained SuperLearner, this is also where you'll begin creating visual mnemonics to be filled in with more detail later.

Next is the Question phase, which happens simultaneously alongside the Survey phase. In this phase, we ask ourselves questions to improve our motivation, such as "For what reason am I reading this?" "What's in it for me?" or "What do I expect to see here?" Doing this helps create curiosity, which in turn generates motivation and enthusiasm for reading. More on that in a bit.

Next, we Read, either by speed-reading or in the normal fashion. When reading, you reap the benefit of the previous S and Q steps, so you do not reread or dwell on irrelevant details.

With reading done, we Recall. We attempt to remember what we've read, and along the way, we create and improve detailed, visual mnemonics. This happens after reading each paragraph, page, or chapter, depending on the density of the material. This is our way to ensure that we actually recall the content we're reading.

Finally, we Review. We analyze the content from multiple perspectives. We assess what we've learned and try and connect it to previous knowledge. We perform spaced repetition on the material for an extended period of time. Believe it or not, the most effective readers spend more time on this step than all previous steps combined. That's because if you don't review the material, both immediately after and in increasing intervals, everything you've done so far is useless. You'll just forget it anyway.

So, now that we understand the SQ3R model overall, let's learn how to optimize it, starting out with the superskill of pre-reading.

THE POWER OF PRE-READING

The skill we call "pre-reading" is actually two processes in one: Surveying and Questioning.

If you look up the verb "survey" in the dictionary, you'll see a few definitions. To survey something means "to investigate, examine, question, and record information about it." That's a fantastic definition because this is exactly what we want to do during pre-reading.

At first, pre-reading may seem counterintuitive to you: Doesn't it add extra steps, slowing you down? Actually, the opposite is true. According to researchers, pre-reading helps us speed up, while priming our brains for reading with higher retention.[9]

How can a quick skim actually improve our reading? First of all, pre-reading enhances our focus and motivation, eliminating drifting off and rereading. At the same time, it actually makes it easier for us to read at higher speeds when we do read. This effect is especially important for dense materials or mixed reading with lots of pictures, like textbooks. How many times have you read a textbook, only to get stuck on a side box in the margins? Typically, these side boxes are there to define terms you don't know or give you some important contextual explanation of a new concept. But breaking your focus in the middle of reading to study them is both slow and ineffective. By first pre-reading the text and any cutaways, we are able to investigate and examine the information we're about to learn. In essence, we are clearing any potential roadblocks that could hinder our reading or comprehension when we reach the first "R."

Pre-reading isn't something we made up in our Super-

9   H. Y. McClusky, "An Experiment on the Influence of Preliminary Skimming on Reading," *Journal of Educational Psychology* 25, no. 7 (Oct 1934): 521–529, http://dx.doi.org/10.1037/h0070829.

Learner courses, though. As I alluded, it's supported by a great number of scientific studies.[10]

So how do you actually do it?

SURVEYING THE SITUATION

When we pre-read a text, we're essentially skimming. But not your normal type of skimming. Instead, we're spending a couple of seconds per page, skimming at a speed of about five to eight times our current reading speed. We are not reading the text—or even trying to. Instead, we're looking for titles, subheadings, proper nouns, numbers, words, or anything that doesn't seem to fit in. When we pre-read, we gain an understanding of the structure of the text, and we build a sort of mental map. If there are "cutaways," or terms that jump out at us as unfamiliar, we stop our pre-reading and gain a better understanding before resuming.

As we go along, we start to generate thoughts, opinions, and ideas about the text. We may think to ourselves, "Oh, this is interesting! They're going to talk about Buzz Aldrin

10 Jessica Marinaccio, "The Most Effective Pre-reading Strategies for Comprehension" (master's thesis, St. John Fisher College, 2012); Minoo Alemi and Saman Ebadi, "The Effects of Pre-reading Activities on ESP Reading Comprehension," *Journal of Language Teaching and Research* 1, no. 5 (September 2010): 569-577, https://doi.org/10.4304/jltr.1.5.569-577; Akbar Azizifara et al., "The Effect of Pre-Reading Activities on the Reading Comprehension Performance of Ilami High School Students," *Procedia - Social and Behavioral Sciences* 192 (June 24, 2015): 188-194, https://doi.org/10.1016/j.sbspro.2015.06.027.

here," for example. These will serve as temporary markers, and we'll be able to upgrade them later with more detailed visual markers after we read the text. The Pareto Principle, or 80/20 rule, is once again very helpful here. In pre-reading, we're looking for that 20 percent of details that give us an 80 percent understanding of what we're going to be reading—or at least what the text is about.

This means that when you actually read the text, all you have to do is fill in the rest of the details. This skill takes time to fully develop, but it's a pivotal one in speed-reading—or reading in general. Practice it diligently, and it will make you a much more effective and focused reader.

Keep in mind that even though you don't register the text at this speed, you are building a map and becoming more familiar with it subconsciously. This is like getting a feel for the layout of a neighborhood by driving through it at forty miles an hour. Don't get frustrated, and don't get hung up on understanding the text. Just understand the flow, and take note of any interesting points that might jump out at you.

This alone is a major benefit of pre-reading, but as we've mentioned, it's not the only one.

QUESTION EVERYTHING

The next step in the SQ3R framework is no less important in pre-reading: questioning.

Remember our dear old friend Dr. Malcolm Knowles and what he taught us? Adult learners must harness prior experience. They also demand a pressing need and an immediate application of what they're learning. In short, adult learners need to be curious about what they're learning. They need to understand how it connects to their existing knowledge. Modern researchers have proven this time and time again. The more we can connect learning to a person's previous knowledge and experience, the better.

As we've mentioned, though, the unfortunate reality is that much of what we read will not fulfill these requirements. Even if we're in a field we love, a lot of the reading we do will not be immediately applicable to us.

Fortunately, if we learn to generate the right types of questions, we can overcome this hurdle altogether. You see, the human brain simply can't resist a good question. We are problem-solving machines. Questions, therefore, cause our brains to fire up and pay attention unlike anything else.

Do you know what else our brains love? Being right! If

you've read anything by behavioral economist Dan Ariely, you know that our brains are prone to all sorts of cognitive biases. One of the most important of these is confirmation bias. This is the tendency to pay extra special attention to things that confirm our beliefs. We do this at the expense of new information that could change the way we think—even if that new information is true. This is normally a really bad thing—especially during election season! But when we pre-read, we can turn this on its head and use it to our advantage. By asking ourselves certain types of questions, which compare new knowledge to our own, we supercharge our focus towards finding out one all-important thing: Are we right, or not? This one trick alone can make even the most boring material, such as tax law, much more interesting.

Perhaps, for example, you see that the text mentions Baltimore, Maryland. Ask yourself: What the heck does Baltimore have to do with tax law? What happened there? Was there a precedent set? Make a predictive assumption, and then, as you read, check to see if your prediction was right. Doing so will make you very motivated to read through the text and figure out just what the heck is going on. While you're at it, you should find things that don't seem to fit in, and ask yourself what they're doing there.

Another effective class of questions is to ask yourself: How will I use this information? As you pre-read the text and begin to get a feel for its contents, try to envision scenarios in which it could affect your life. Imagine how you could benefit from having that knowledge. How could you use this knowledge in your day-to-day life? Who are some people in your life with whom you could share it? When might it be useful for sparking up a conversation? It sounds basic, but simply giving your brain this "why" is often the difference between intently focusing and feeling your eyes glaze over.

When I was struggling with pre-reading training, my mentors and coaches, Anna and Lev, offered me a tip that has stuck with me to this day. They challenged me to consider questions of perspective—mine, the author's, or even third parties'. Though we are not yet reading the text itself, we are seeing keywords, and those keywords are enough to generate some pretty opinion-laden questions.

These include:

- What viewpoint do I anticipate the author taking?
- What viewpoint do I have going into reading this article?
- Where might the author be wrong?
- Where am I open to being persuaded on this topic?
- How could this material be improved?
- What would critics of this article likely say?
- Who might agree or disagree with what this article likely says?

- What would I expect to see in this text that I am not seeing at this speed?

As with all pre-reading questions, these thought exercises are designed to put your cognitive biases on "high alert." When you finally read the text, you'll find that you have a laser-like focus and determination to prove yourself right—no matter how boring the text may be.

You might wonder how one can generate all these questions without actually reading the chapter. In reality, it's pretty easy. Let's say, for example, you were pre-reading an article about nutrition. Just by noting a few prominent keywords, such as "paleo," "grains," "animal protein," "cancer," "obesity," or "insulin," I can already tell a lot. And by seeing which studies and which experts are cited, I can tell even more.

Before I even read the article, I can assume what stance the author is going to take. Based on that, I definitely know whether I agree or don't. I may think of a few of my vegetarian or vegan friends at the same time and consider whether they'll turn blue in the face or love every word. I'll even consider where I feel the author may be biased, misinformed, or just plain wrong.

As you can see, once you've completed your initial pass-through of pre-reading, you'll have a lot of questions you're eager to answer. This has a massive effect on concentration, comprehension, and retention. If you suffer from attention deficit disorder, as I do, you know that if you really want to know something, you can be laser focused. After generating all these perspectives and questions, you will be just that.

If you really want to know why on earth Baltimore is in this text, you'll focus harder than you ever imagined you'd focus on tax law.

Many students flock to our accelerated learning programs to 10X their memory or triple their reading speed. But the truth is, I often feel that pre-reading is one of the most valuable "Easter eggs" in the SuperLearner method. People rarely anticipate it making as big of a difference as it does, and best of all, it's something you can implement today, with little to no practice.

Try it out on the next chapter of this book, and you'll see what I mean. Place your finger on the first page of the chapter (or open the "X-Ray" feature on your Kindle). Then, flip through the pages at an extremely high speed. As you do, start asking yourself questions about the details you're noticing.

The results will surprise you.

From now on, I suggest that you pre-read just about everything. While I might not use pre-reading for a suspenseful fiction book (spoiler alert!), this skill is useful in everything from long emails to blog posts and even scientific textbooks.

What are you waiting for? Turn the page and try it out.

CHAPTER 10

LEARNING TO WALK ON YOUR HANDS

———

At various points throughout my academic career, I attempted to learn to "speed-read." I read Evelyn Wood's famous book on speed-reading. I tried "The PX Method." And, indeed, when I fatefully met Lev in 2011, I was able to read at an impressive 450 words per minute (wpm).

The problem? My comprehension rate was about 40 percent.

Lev, on the other hand, was able to read nearly twice as fast as I was—with comprehension in the 80- to 90-percent range. In retrospect, this isn't surprising. Unlike me, Lev had the memory and pre-reading tools that you now have. And soon, you'll have the speed-reading tools, as well.

* * *

Before we go into the "flashy" and "sexy" skill of pre-reading, I want to manage your expectations. When we talk about speed-reading, we are not talking about "photographing" a page per second. We're not talking about reading one page with each eye, or reading speeds of 5,000 wpm. While all that sounds nice, the fact is, science has pretty much proven that none of those things are even remotely possible.

Disappointing, I know.

But here's the interesting and exciting part. The most exhaustive research "disproving" speed-reading does so by demonstrating that comprehension begins to drop off at 600 wpm, and declines steeply at 700 to 800 wpm.[11] To put this into perspective, the average college-educated reader reads 200 to 250 wpm in English. When viewed in this light, it seems to me that "speed-reading" is very much possible—but only in the ranges of 600 to 800 wpm.

For a much more detailed analysis of the research, please visit http://superhumanacademy.com/science.

How, then, do we speed-read?

---

11 Keith Rayner et al., "So Much to Read, So Little Time: How Do We Read, and Can Speed Reading Help?" *Psychological Science in the Public Interest* 17, no. 1 (January 14, 2016): 4-34, https://doi.org/10.1177/1529100615623267.

Well, the basics of it are quite simple. I will explain them to you, you will read my explanation, and then you will begin to practice. But speed-reading is a lot like learning to walk on your hands—which, after a year or two of practice, I learned to do quite comfortably. Knowing what to do and being able to do it effectively are two very different things. And it will always be much more comfortable and natural to walk on your feet when you get out of bed in the morning.

Speed-reading is very much the same. Without a doubt, the memory and pre-reading skills you've learned so far are a complete overhaul to the way you think and learn. But over the years, I've come to realize that speed-reading is a specific tool useful for specific scenarios. Would I speed-read a nice novel before bed? Probably not. But did I speed-read a bunch of academic research to write this chapter? You bet.

What's more, after decades of reading the "slow" way, be prepared for speed-reading to feel unnatural and downright exhausting. Another metaphor I like to share with students is that of slouching. Though we all know that we should sit up straight (or better yet, switch to a standing desk), I bet 90 percent of you just corrected yourselves upon reading this sentence. Speed-reading is a lot like this. Oftentimes, when I sit down to read, I must "remind" myself to speed-read. This ties in with the skill we previously learned, proper preparation and mindset. Once I've determined why I'm reading a text, I can determine whether or not speed-reading is appropriate.

And now, let's learn how to actually do it.

SUBVOCALIZATION

For as long as speed-reading has been around, experts have taught that one of the keys to reading faster is to eliminate subvocalization. In other words, get rid of that pesky "voice" in your head. After all, that voice can really only speak at a pace of about 400 to 450 wpm. Your brain, by contrast, can recognize complex images, symbols, and situations in as little as 0.013 seconds. Subvocalizing what we read is like trying to describe a photo to someone instead of just showing it to them. It takes high-fidelity visual information and degrades it to low-bandwidth auditory information. If we eliminate the voice, we eliminate the bottleneck, right?

The truth is, it's not quite so simple. Because of the way we process language, research shows us that it's impossible to eliminate subvocalization entirely. We can, however, dramatically minimize it and learn to subvocalize only a small portion of the words we read. Doing so yields a great improvement to our ability to read quickly, albeit a very difficult one. In our programs, we call this "breaking the sound barrier," and just like getting up to Mach speeds, it's something you need to work up to.

LARGER FIXATIONS

For a moment, pay special attention to the way you are reading this page. While you may think that your eyes are moving smoothly, in reality, they are not. In fact, they cannot. Our eyes are literally incapable of making smooth, consistent movements unless we're tracking a moving object. To try this out, look at the beginning of this line, and try to smoothly move your eyes from one end to the other. You might think your eyes are moving in one fluid motion, but in fact, this transition is completed in many tiny, rapid movements. If you're curious, compare these movements with smooth ones by waving a finger in front of your eyes and following it. See the difference?

When gazing at sets of stationary objects, our eyes focus in fixations. Each time your eyes focus lock focus on something, that's a fixation. The fast, precise movements from one fixation to another are known as saccades. Here's the kicker. To keep our vision stable and prevent us from getting disoriented, our brains actually "shut off" our vision while our eyes are in motion. Then, unbeknownst to us, they stitch the pictures back together when we settle on a new fixation. This phenomenon is called saccadic masking or saccadic blindness, and it means that for a significant portion of the time you are looking at this page, your eyes aren't actually inputting any additional information to your brain.

Unfortunately, there's not much we can do about saccadic blindness. What we can do is reduce the amount of time we spend in it. A normal reader is trained to make one fixation per word, resulting in about eight to ten fixations per line. That's a lot of time spent in saccadic blindness. But if we can train ourselves only to make, say, one or two fixations per line, we spend much less time in saccadic blindness. In this way, we can absorb more information—faster.

We train to do this using a tool called a Schultz table.

NEW GAME		Next Value: 1		Timer: 57
1	13	24	17	8
10	5	23	20	12
9	4	3	14	2
16	6	25	11	15
7	18	19	21	22

Schultz tables contain a grid of numbers similar to a completed Soduku puzzle. To use one, you simply stare into the middle box and attempt to "see" what is outside of your immediate focus. This trains you to not only recognize what is in the very middle of your focus—the fovea—but also to pick up on the blurry periphery of your vision—the parafovea.

This is admittedly a bit controversial. On the one hand, the research is clear that speed-readers' claims of being able to "preview" a subsequent line are absolute bunk. On the other hand, numerous studies have demonstrated that hiding the text immediately after the reader's fovea severely impacts reading speed and comprehension.[12]

---

12 Dennis F. Fisher and Wayne L. Shebilske, *Eye Movements in Reading* (Cambridge, MA: Academic Press, 1983), 153–179, https://doi.org/10.1016/B978-0-12-583680-7.50014-X; Keith Rayner et al., "Raeding Wrods With Jubmled Lettres: There Is a Cost," *Psychological Science* 17, no. 3 (March 1, 2006): 192–193, http://dx.doi.org/10.1111/j.1467-9280.2006.01684.x.

From this, we know that readers clearly use information from more than just the fixated word to read effectively.[13] So no, you won't be able to read two lines at a time, or even one full line at a time. But you can benefit from learning to capture a line in just two or three fixations, with two to four words per fixation.

OPTIMIZED FIXATIONS

Once you've learned to take in words in larger groups of two to four, you'll inevitably notice that a lot of your first and last fixations are somewhat wasteful. As my father always liked to joke when I struggled with my reading material, "Make sure you're reading the black stuff, not the white stuff." Most readers center their fovea on the first letter of the first word and the last letter of the last word in a line. Doing so means that half of your focal range is wasted on blank, white paper. Of course, there's very little information in the margins—until you write it in there. For this reason, the most advanced speed-readers center their fixations on the second and second to last words on a line, like so:

---

13   Rayner et al., "So Much to Read, So Little Time," 4–34.

But I must explain to you how all this mistaken idea of denouncing of a pleasure and praising pain was born and I will give you a complete account of the system, and expound the actual teachings of the great explorer of the truth, the master-builder of human happiness. No one rejects, dislikes, or avoids pleasure itself, because it is pleasure, but because those who do not know how to pursue pleasure rationally encounter consequences that are extremely painful. Nor again is there anyone who loves or pursues or desires to obtain pain of itself, because it is pain, but occasionally circumstances occur in which toil and pain can procure him some great pleasure. To take a trivial example, which of us ever undertakes laborious physical exercise, except to obtain some advantage from it? But who has any right to find fault with a man who chooses to enjoy a pleasure that has no annoying consequences, or one who avoids a pain that produces no resultant pleasure?

On the other hand, we denounce with righteous indignation and dislike men who are so beguiled and demoralized by the charms of pleasure of the moment, so blinded by desire, that they cannot foresee the pain and trouble that are bound to ensue; and equal blame belongs to those who fail

And, quite honestly, that's all there is to it.

It all sounds easy enough, right? It's not. This skill alone takes students months to learn, and the truth is, if you don't use it, it gets rusty.

For this reason, we advocate learning with an approach called progressive overload. Originally taken from the world of weight-lifting, progressive overload means training just at the cusp of your capability and adjusting as soon as you are comfortable at a certain level.

PROGRESSIVE OVERLOAD

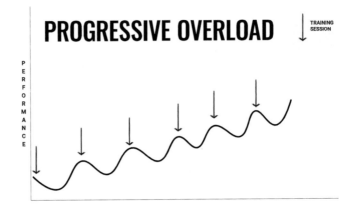

In speed-reading, this means reading at a speed where you can just barely comprehend. Many speed-reading courses would tell you to begin reading at a speed of 600 wpm or beyond. But doing so gives your comprehension no opportunity to gradually improve. This is why I encourage you to gradually level up. Think about it: at the gym, you wouldn't go straight to lifting 450 pounds. You would lift a weight that is challenging to lift only once or twice, right? Then, you'd only increase the weight once you were able to effectively lift it five times. So, too, should you train for speed-reading.

When you're first starting out, it's helpful to cover what you've read with an index card, using it to set a pace based on the speed you want to go. Initially, this may mean reading just 350 wpm. To do this, figure out how many seconds that is per page. It will likely be around fifty seconds for your average book. Then, give yourself approximately that much time to read the page.

At first, you will feel that you are hardly comprehending anything. This is normal. In fact, when you're learning, it's a good idea to stop and "quiz" yourself on what you read. Stop at the end of a section or chapter and list out the details you have absorbed. Then, flip back through the book to see how you did. With time, your comprehension will improve, and you'll begin to feel that you're comprehending much more than you were before. This is a good indication that it's time to take your speed up a notch.

As you juggle all this, don't forget everything you've learned thus far. Before reading, pre-read the chapter ahead, survey its structure, and generate your questions. After speed-reading each paragraph or page, pause, and take a moment to recall, creating visual markers to represent what you learned. Once you've finished the chapter, close the book and review those visual markers. And of course, revisit the books you've read with some form of spaced repetition. Unless you complete each of these steps—particularly the memory aspects—you will have no more success than I did before discovering this method.

If this seems like a lot, don't worry. We have put together a "flight checklist" that you can print out and keep with you. It will remind you of all the things you need to do before, during, and after you speed-read. That way, you won't neglect any of these important steps in the process. You can download that worksheet by visiting http://jle.vi/bonus.

Speed-reading may take a few weeks—even months—of practice to completely master. Don't despair. Take it slow, gradually increase your speed, and continue training. One day, it will simply "click" for you. You'll break the sound barrier and realize that you're absorbing information at speeds of up to 700 wpm.

In that moment, rejoice! But remember, if you don't use this newfound skill, you will lose it.

CHAPTER 11

CROSS-POLLINATION AND BRUTE FORCE LEARNING

———

"Who is wise? He that learns from everyone."

—JEWISH PROVERB

Now that your passion for learning is matched by your ability to learn quickly and easily, you're likely to go crazy like a tourist at a buffet. New sources, new subjects, new books, new courses. It's all so exciting! And just as I did after Anna and Lev's course, you'll probably dive in head first, devouring everything in sight, and jumping around like a monkey from tree to tree.

Many students, myself included, tend to beat themselves up about this. One of the biggest "complaints" I hear from students is that they're unable to focus in on one subject, book, course, or field. "If I could just finish what I started, then I could go on to learning the next thing. Why can't I just focus?"

But what if I told you that there's actually a great deal of benefit to jumping around? Or that it's not only okay to learn multiple subjects from multiple sources, but that it's actually preferred?

First, let's start with the simpler version of this behavior: jumping from subject to subject. In my peak learning phases, when my workload was lighter, I'd jump around and learn a different subject every day. One day, I'd be obsessed with Russian. The next, I'd spend hours tinkering away on the piano. On the weekend, I might devour an entire biography in one sitting, practice Olympic weight lifting, or spend six hours in the park learning AcroYoga.

What a mess, right?

Well, in reality, what I came to realize is this: learning anything helps you learn everything.

First off, learning unique new subjects exposes you to all different types of knowledge. This, in turn, expands your mind's ability to take in new information. From the outside, music is so seemingly different from, say, acrobatics or law. Thus, casting a wide net and learning a diverse set of subjects develops a broader set of skills for learning. What's more, as a SuperLearner, it gives you more anchor points of pre-existing knowledge to connect to. To someone who has never studied a foreign language or a musical instrument before, learning one is a monumental task. But to someone who already speaks or plays four, it's a lot easier. There's just so much crossover.

It's important to note, though, that this crossover is not limited to knowledge in the same field. After all, the whole of human knowledge is in some way connected. It's nearly impossible to learn something without it carrying over into other types of learning. When I decided to learn AcroYoga, a form of partner acrobatics that involves dazzling poses, flips, and routines, I didn't know the first thing about it. But I did know plenty about Olympic weight lifting, hand balancing, and kinesiology. Because of this, I was able to "carry over" a lot of my knowledge and radically condense my learning curve. All I had to do was make use of my understandings of weight transfer, biomechanics, and balance into this seemingly foreign field of study. It wasn't long before I became quite the accomplished AcroYogi.

In the SuperLearner methodology, we refer to this as cross-pollination. Cross-pollination states that learning one subject will have significant, unforeseen benefits when learning another. This is not only a reason to learn as much as you can about as many things as you can; it's a strategy you can use to your own advantage. Want to become a better golfer? Put down the clubs and pick up a book on biomechanics, physics, or kinesiology. Want to be a better negotiator? Take a couple courses on body language, psychology, or mirror neurons. The examples are endless.

But there's another important benefit of cross-pollination. It allows us to take advantage of our enthusiasm and passion for learning in real time. As we've discussed, sometimes in life we must learn things we are less than enthusiastic about. Why, then, suppress our passion, motivation, and enthusiasm for learning when they do present themselves? If you're not excited about studying guitar today and are longing to watch that foreign language movie, I say do it! The motivation and drive to learn are precious resources, and so when you feel them within yourself, take advantage!

Cross-pollination encourages us to jump from subject to subject more freely—but what about within subjects? When I began studying Russian, I couldn't home in and focus on just one source of learning. There were just too many options to choose from! Online courses, podcasts, textbooks, blog posts, flash cards, meetup groups. Heck, I even began watching the Russian version of *Winnie The Pooh* to see what I could learn (if you need a good laugh, I highly, highly recommend it). Certainly, doing so hindered my progress, right? I mean, wouldn't it have been better to pick just one book and read it start to finish?

No way! As we learn, our brains are forming complex neural networks of everything we know and understand about a subject. And no matter how good a particular book, course, or tutor is, nobody and nothing is comprehensive enough to stand completely on its own. Think about it this way: though kale is certainly very healthy for you, you'd be hard-pressed to find a doctor advocating the "nothing but kale" diet. Holistic nutrition, like holistic learning, requires a great deal of variety—even within the same subject matter. Even if a particular resource seems exhaustive, you still stand to gain from approaching a subject in as many different ways as possible. Why? Because different people understand, present, and explain the exact same concept in very different ways. As a learner, it's impossible to know if the way that you're first exposed to is what's going to "click" for you.

I'll never forget the way I learned about one particularly confusing concept in Advanced Corporate Finance. One afternoon, I stepped out of the lecture hall at INSEAD, one of the world's top business schools. I'd just listened to my professor explain the concept in depth for over an hour. You'd think that I would have completely understood the subject, right? After all, this particular professor had literally written the textbook on it! He was one of the world's foremost experts on the topic! And yet, I was more confused than ever. Neither the textbook nor the lecture made the slightest bit of sense to me. Not sure what to do, I went into the library, put on my headphones, and pulled up the completely free website khanacademy.com. There, the same concept was explained in an entirely different way, which, to me, was much, much clearer. Within fifteen minutes, I understood the subject in its entirety. Was my professor a bad teacher? Not at all. It just so happened that the way he understood and explained the subject was not a way that would ever make sense to me as a student. Had I persisted in trying to learn it his way, I might still be sitting in that classroom with my head in my hands.

In the SuperLearner methodology, we call this approach brute force learning. It's a term I learned from the incredibly clever entrepreneur Mattan Griffel. Mattan himself lifted the term "brute force" from the world of computer hacking. In that context, to "brute force" something means to attack it from as many different perspectives as possible to try and gain complete access. Brute force learning, on the other hand, means learning something from as many different perspectives as possible to try and gain complete understanding.

Doing this has a number of powerful benefits. First off, the more you approach something from different perspectives, the better, more holistic understanding you'll have of it. If you think about the things in life you've mastered, it's unlikely you did so by simply reading one book or attending one lecture on them. That's because the first time you're exposed to a new idea, your brain is still forming a fuzzy understanding of how it fits into your worldview. After all, you have no pre-existing knowledge to connect it to. You are grasping at straws, trying to find ways to link it up to the things you already know. But over time, with repeated and increasingly detailed exposure, your brain is able to figure out where the details fit into the bigger picture. It's able to connect each new piece of information to the rest of your knowledge, creating stronger neural networks, and therefore, a much more complete understanding.

What's more, as Mattan notes, brute force learning teaches us that it's okay not to understand something the first time we learn it. This itself has unforeseen benefits. As we already know, the more spaced repetition and overlearning we do, the more likely we are to remember the information long term. Brute force learning, then, is also a way to overlearn, without the monotony of rereading the same textbook or rewatching the same lecture. Overall, learning this way takes a lot of the pressure out of learning and prevents us from feeling "dumb" if we don't get it immediately.

I sure wish I knew about this little trick when I was in middle school!

The next time you prepare to learn something, don't confine yourself to learning monogamously! As you build your learning plan, make sure to include numerous sources, perspectives, and peripheral subjects. Go on tangents, and get lost in the weeds! This not only fulfills yet another requirement of Dr. Malcolm Knowles—self-concept. It will also result in better overall understanding—and a lot less boredom and frustration.

CHAPTER 12

CHECK YOURSELF

—

"You can fool yourself, you know.

You'd think it's impossible, but it turns out it's the easiest thing of all."

—JODI PICOULT, *VANISHING ACTS*

Often in life, we lie to ourselves more than anyone else. We tell ourselves that we'll wake up early and go to the gym—knowing full well that it's probably not going to happen. For the most part, these little "white lies" are not only normal, they are a valuable skill to have. Being able to "lie" to ourselves that everything is going to be okay, that things happen for a reason, or that some seemingly bad occurrence will turn out for the best is a huge part of emotional resilience. Psychologists call this "cognitive reframing," and it's one of the best techniques out there for being a happier, more grounded person.

When it comes to learning, though, this ability to lie to ourselves can hinder our progress. In many cases, we believe that we have learned something, but in fact, we haven't—at least not to the level we would like.

In the 1940s, educational psychologist Benjamin Bloom and his team began developing a hierarchy of learning. They knew that simply remembering something was very different from actually understanding it. And of course, being able to think critically about it was something very different still. Over the next sixteen years, Bloom and his colleagues revised and refined the framework. In 1956, they published *Taxonomy of Educational Objectives*, better known as Bloom's Taxonomy.

Since then, Bloom's Taxonomy has served as the backbone of many different philosophies of education. In fact, researchers and students of Bloom's have continued refining the theory, with an updated edition published in 2001.

At its basic level, Bloom's Taxonomy looks like this:

BLOOM'S TAXONOMY

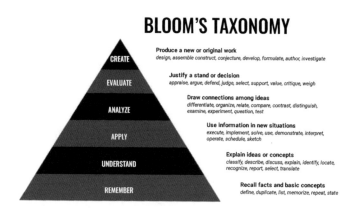

CREATE — Produce a new or original work
design, assemble construct, conjecture, develop, formulate, author, investigate

EVALUATE — Justify a stand or decision
appraise, argue, defend, judge, select, support, value, critique, weigh

ANALYZE — Draw connections among ideas
differentiate, organize, relate, compare, contrast, distinguish, examine, experiment, question, test

APPLY — Use information in new situations
execute, implement, solve, use, demonstrate, interpret, operate, schedule, sketch

UNDERSTAND — Explain ideas or concepts
classify, describe, discuss, explain, identify, locate, recognize, report, select, translate

REMEMBER — Recall facts and basic concepts
define, duplicate, list, memorize, repeat, state

At the base of the pyramid, we start with "remember," the ability to recall something from memory at a basic level. Take note, though, of what is not at the base of this pyramid: "recognize." You know that feeling when something is on the tip of your tongue and you aren't able to recall it till someone gives you the answer? "Yes! That's the one!" you say. This is recognition. But recognition is quite different from recall. To actually know something, we have to be able not just to recognize it, but to apply higher-level thinking towards it. One can only assume that for this reason, "recognize" didn't make the cut.

As you move up the pyramid, you'll find increasingly complex levels of thinking. Once we remember a piece of information, the next step is to actually understand it. Can we classify the type of knowledge it represents, or explain it in our own words? Can we discuss it with others?

Once we can, the step after that is to actually apply it. We all know a lot of very "book smart" people who can tell you all the facts and figures. But when it comes time to get their hands dirty, they're more talk than anything. That's because to actually apply something takes an even higher level of knowledge. It takes knowing when and how it can be used. This also marks an important transition between theoretical and applied knowledge. Hopefully, it's the latter that we aspire to.

Here's where things get really advanced. Next up on the taxonomy is "analyze." Can we look critically at this piece of information, comparing and contrasting it to other information or ideas? Can we examine it in enough depth to break it down to its essential parts and come up with unique ways of thinking about it?

At this point, we thoroughly understand the material both as a whole and in its individual components. Now, we must ask: Are we able to evaluate it? Are we competent enough to actually critique it, weigh its validity, support its arguments, or dismiss it altogether?

The utmost level in Bloom's Taxonomy, and the reason for the big shakeup in 2001, is "create." It's one thing to understand the thinking or ideas of another, or even to criticize and evaluate them. It's an entirely different thing to create your own original thoughts. In this stage, we know enough about a topic to develop our own related works. At the most basic level, this is the difference between being a music aficionado and composing your own music. At the highest levels, it's the difference between a master's degree and a PhD. One demands only the study and analysis of other people's ideas, while the other requires you to contribute original thinking of your own.

Bloom's Taxonomy is a helpful reminder that the words "learning," "knowing," and "understanding" greatly oversimplify what's really going on. In fact, it's reminiscent of an apocryphal story about theoretical physicist Max Planck. After winning the Nobel Prize, Planck toured Germany, giving the same standard lecture on the new quantum mechanics. After a while, his chauffeur had memorized the lecture and asked Planck if they could switch places for a day. On the big day, Planck sat in the audience in a chauffeur's cap, and his driver delivered the lecture flawlessly on stage. After the lecture, however, a physics professor stood up and asked a detailed, complex question. The chauffeur's response? "I'm surprised to receive such an elementary question in an advanced city like Munich. I'm going to let my chauffeur reply!"

But how do we actually determine how far along we are in any given subject? How do we know if we have Planck-level knowledge or just chauffeur-level memory?

In other words, how can we avoid the traps of believing we've mastered a subject, only to realize we're in the early stages of our understanding?

The answer, of course, is to test ourselves, in a variety of practical ways.

Testing gets a really bad rap—and it probably should, given the way it's conducted in most schools today. Students study only what's on the exam, forgetting it almost immediately thereafter. Worse yet, exams are often multiple-choice format, which requires only recognizing the correct answer. And in all but a few subjects, it's rare that an exam requires original or creative thinking.

In reality, certain types of testing can be extremely powerful tools in your learning tool kit. Plenty of research has demonstrated that self-quizzing and collaborative group quizzes significantly improve learning.[14] One study at Purdue University found that tests requiring inference and high-level comprehension were even more effective than continued study![15] In fact, in 2008, another group of researchers compared two different strategies for learn-

---

14 Mario Vázquez-García, "Collaborative-Group Testing Improves Learning and Knowledge Retention of Human Physiology Topics in Second-Year Medical Students," *Advances in Physiology Education* 42, no. 2 (June 1, 2018): 232-239, http://dx.doi.org/10.1152/advan.00113.2017.

15 Jeffrey D. Karpickea and Janell R. Blunt, "Retrieval Practice Produces More Learning than Elaborative Studying with Concept Mapping," *Science* 331, no. 6018 (February 11, 2011): 772-775, http://dx.doi.org/10.1126/science.1199327.

ing new vocabulary. One group was instructed to quiz themselves, while the other was told to continue studying and reviewing. The results were pretty astonishing: the students who quizzed themselves remembered up to 80 percent more words![16]

Of course, nobody expects you to spend half of your learning time developing quizzes to test your own knowledge. Doing so would be impractical—and really boring. Furthermore, the types of "basic" tests that you'd develop would likely be no better than simply testing yourself using flashcards. Alternatively, you could probably find ready-made quizzes online. You might just be able to find some publicly-available university exams or even free quizzes on learning websites. Without a doubt, this is one of the best ways you can improve your learning using testing.

But let's be honest: How likely are you to actually sit and take an exam that you don't have to?

Yeah. I don't blame you.

How, then, can we leverage the advantages of testing

---

16   Jeffrey D. Karpicke and Henry L. Roediger III, "The Critical Importance of Retrieval for Learning," *Science* 319, no. 5865 (February 15, 2008): 966-968, http://dx.doi.org/10.1126/science.1152408.

without reliving the trauma of our high school or university days?

I'd like to once again remind you of our dear old friend, Dr. Malcolm Knowles. As Knowles discovered, adults learn much more effectively when we have an immediate application and a pressing need for whatever it is we're learning. This, more than the actual format of the test, is probably why studies show testing to be such a boon to learning. After all, as the saying goes, "Learning is not a spectator sport." So why not develop our own "tests" in ways that are fast, fun, and effective?

Let's say you're learning a musical instrument, and you wish to improve by a certain amount. You could always hire a private tutor to "test" your knowledge of the piano. But in reality, this will be much less rigorous than a form of testing that requires analysis, critical thinking, or even your own creation. What if you instead committed to testing your skills by learning a friend's favorite song for their birthday? Better yet, what if you committed to composing an original piece for them? Now that would be a powerful test of everything you've learned, from key signatures to tempo, and it's bound to be more rewarding than some boring online quiz.

Years ago, I interviewed famed Irish polyglot Benny Lewis, author of the book *Fluent in 3 Months*. When asked for some of his best language learning hacks, Benny shared a technique that has stuck with me to this day. In his method, Benny advocates speaking a language from day one—even if you only know a few words. Forget studying and studying until you are "ready" to debut your language skills. Benny advises that you get out there and test yourself immediately by speaking to native speakers in an ongoing loop of learn, test, learn, test.

I love this idea.

First of all, it really raises the stakes. When you speak from day one, you feel constantly tested by your conversation partners. This, in turn, provides a huge amount of near-instant feedback in a way that you can remember. Think about it this way. If you wanted to get better at bowling but were forced to bowl in the dark, which would you prefer: Bowling an entire game blindly, and reviewing your results at the end, or switching on the lights after each round to course correct as you go? Most likely, you'd opt to get more frequent feedback as soon as possible. So why don't we make the same decision when learning new material?

Whereas I accidentally spent months learning unnecessary words in Russian, Benny Lewis was able to immediately assess which words he was missing via real-world interactions. Whereas I unknowingly overlooked a major aspect of Russian grammar, Benny discovered it in an early conversation. Each time Benny "tests" himself in this way, he notes the words or grammatical structures he's lacking. This is a lot like a student studying their own mistakes on a practice exam—if there were an exam to study from every day. This dramatically accelerates Benny's progress and ensures that every minute he spends actually studying is well spent.

For my full interview with Benny Lewis and a list of my favorite places to find language partners, visit http://jle.vi/bonus.

Done this way, "testing" yourself can not only be fast but also fun. It need not feel like a "waste" of time; it can be practical and useful. Sure, subjecting yourself to a more traditional form of "testing" is certainly advisable and is definitely worth doing, if you can bear it. With that said, I encourage you to take a broader view of what "testing" means. If you're learning a programming language, test yourself by actually building something with the new concepts you're learning. If you're learning a new instrument, test yourself by performing for others. There are so many ways to engineer self-testing into your learning routine. You just have to be creative and opportunistic. Even a conversation among friends can be a powerful way to test your knowledge.

If you're hoping to learn a subject, another great way to

"test" yourself is to write—and publish—a blog post about it. For that matter, there's one form of self-testing that goes above and beyond the benefits of any other: teaching others.

CHAPTER 13

PAY IT FORWARD

———

"To teach is to learn twice over."

—JOSEPH JOUBERT

You've probably heard the popular saying, "Once taught, twice learned." The idea is simple: when we teach other people, we reinforce our own learning. But did you know that this idea is not only supported by neuroscience—it's also the secret weapon behind some of history's most gifted thinkers?

The idea that teaching others helps us learn has been attributed to many people throughout history. Perhaps the first among them was Roman philosopher and Stoic Seneca the Younger, who said "docendo discimus," or "by teaching, we learn." But this isn't just theoretical. In the modern era, studies have found that the act of teaching causes observable increases in both learning and IQ.

Because of this, neuroscientists have sought to understand exactly how this effect works. More importantly, they've tried to figure out how we can harness it to our own learning advantage. They've studied first-born children, student teachers, and even middle school students in computer teaching simulations.

The results have been both surprising and conclusive: when we teach others, we ourselves benefit tremendously.

But why?

First of all, teaching others is an incredible motivator. The moment we commit to teaching something to someone else, we are compelled to improve our own understanding. Suddenly, we are inspired to serve that person as best we can. Not to mention, we'd like to avoid embarrassing ourselves in the process! This, in effect, harnesses all the benefits of self-testing but makes the stakes real. It's also why, during the chapter on pre-reading, I suggested imagining how you'd share the information with someone you know.

But far beyond that, teaching a subject to someone who knows less than we do presents unique challenges and opportunities for us as learners. Other people have different learning styles, curiosities, and levels of understanding. Consequently, teaching them requires us to take a more thorough and comprehensive approach to our own learning. It requires that we move higher up in Bloom's Taxonomy. We're forced to imagine new and alternative ways to understand a subject. Then, we must create simpler, more creative ways to transmit that understanding to others. This process of dissecting a subject well enough to explain it results in a much deeper understanding among those who teach. As Albert Einstein, who was himself a professor at Princeton, once said on teaching, "If you can't explain it simply, you don't understand it well enough."

Finally, when we teach other people, we are presented with unique questions. These questions are sometimes far outside our own scope of focus. But that doesn't make them any less crucial to our own understanding. Not long ago, I was chatting with a few friends who had developed an interest in Blockchain technology—a subject I'd spent six months intensely SuperLearning. As such, the first half of the conversation entailed me simplifying the inner-workings of this complex innovation. After about twenty minutes of me pontificating, my friend interjected with a highly specific question. So specific, in fact, that "I don't know" was an understatement. I had never even thought about that aspect of the technology! I was immediately motivated to go seek out the answer. Once I did, I was able to fill a knowledge gap I would've never discovered on my own. This illustrates one of the greatest benefits of teaching: the people we teach unknowingly test us. They give us insights into what we don't even know we don't know.

In essence, teaching is a lot like having other people "check your work." When you teach, you share the information you've acquired to the best of your understanding. This isn't that different from a free writing test, in that it requires plenty of higher-level thinking and understanding. As you teach, you are essentially recruiting other people to look for the holes in your knowledge. When they find those holes, they alert you to the areas you should go back and study further. Best of all, they do this in a much more friendly way than a teacher grading your exam, and they do it completely for free! In fact, if you work it out right, they might even pay you to tutor them!

In my years of teaching online, I've come to realize just how powerful it is to have thousands of people highlighting the details I don't fully understand or haven't fully considered. Every time someone asks a question in one of my courses, I'm prompted to ask myself if I understand this aspect of the subject well enough to explain it. If I don't, I'm immediately motivated to do the research and learn about it. In fact, until someone asked me about the effects of teaching and learning, I'd never even thought to check the research behind this learning super-strategy.

In this way, I credit my students for a large portion of the content in my flagship SuperLearner MasterClass.

Teaching is such an effective way to learn that I'll often build entire courses because I want to learn more about the topic myself. This gives me an opportunity to partner up with other experts, download as much of their knowledge as I can, and research whatever else I want to know. Best of all, I get to help students and readers like yourself in the process. Indeed, after mnemonic techniques and speed-reading, teaching has probably had the biggest effect on my ability to learn. I've used it to learn everything from Bitcoin to AcroYoga, endocrine health to marketing. This is why, if we ever meet, you'll probably find me teaching.

This technique was leveraged by many great learners before I was even born. Perhaps best known was Nobel Prize-winning theoretical physicist Dr. Richard Feynman. Feynman had a lifelong passion for teaching, which was evident to anyone who ever met him. Throughout his career, Feynman taught at both Cornell and Caltech. He also advocated for alternative teaching methods at the California State Curriculum Commission and the National Science Teachers Association.

To this day, Feynman is known for his four-step model of learning, which goes like this:

1. Pick a topic you want to understand, and start studying it. Write down everything you know about the topic on a notebook page. Use illustrations wherever possible to simplify your understanding and portrayal of the subject. Add to that page every time you learn something new about it.
2. Pretend to teach your topic to a classroom. Make sure you're able to explain the topic in simple terms.
3. Go back to the books when you get stuck. The gaps in your knowledge should be obvious. Revisit problem areas until you can explain the topic fully.
4. Simplify and use analogies. Repeat the process, continually simplifying your language and connecting facts with analogies. Do this as many times as needed to strengthen your understanding.

Using this methodology, Feynman became one of the most prominent and respected scientists of all time. He was so much more than a Nobel Prize-winning thought leader in one of the most complex subjects known to man, astrophysics. He was also the author of the most popular series of physics lectures and books ever created, *The Feynman Lectures on Physics*. This and his passion for teaching earned him the loving nickname "the great explainer." What's more, Feynman was a tried-and-true polymath. Throughout his life, he used this technique to master not only physics but everything from lockpicking to languages, bongo drums, and even salsa dancing.

As we near the end of our time together, I'd like to make one humble request: teach those around you what you've learned in this book!

One of the best things you can do to reinforce everything you've learned about memory and neuroscience is to get out there and teach it to others.

Tell your kids. Tell your friends. Tell your spouse. Tell anyone who is interested how they can use visual mnemonics and things like the memory palace to learn anything faster. Not only will you be doing them a great service by exposing them to this life-changing field, but you'll also benefit a great deal for all the reasons mentioned above. You might not be a perfect teacher. You might even be new to teaching. But if you've made it this far, you're more than qualified to share these lessons with your friends and family. And if they want to learn more, or they drive you crazy with their questions, send them to http://jle.vi/book, where they can claim a free copy of this book for themselves!

CHAPTER 14

HIGH-PERFORMANCE HABITS

———

Years ago, I became positively obsessed with the skill of hand balancing. I started out by perfecting the standard handstand, but that wasn't nearly enough. In time, I had moved on to the coveted "straddle press." It took eight months, but I finally learned to transition from a high splits into a handstand—without bending my knees or elbows. If it sounds difficult, it's because it is. And when that wasn't enough, I began working my way towards the near impossible: standing on one hand.

Along about this time, I began noticing that both my strength and my balance seemed to vary significantly from day to day. On some days, I had the strength and agility to press up into a perfect handstand and shift my weight back and forth. But on others, I couldn't even get my feet off the ground without cheating and bending my elbows. These variances were due to all kinds of factors: how well I'd slept, how well I'd eaten, how hard my last workout was, and whether I'd consumed alcohol recently. The point is this: never before, in my years of weight lifting or playing sports, had I noticed such significant variance in my ability to perform. Now, however, in this new and challenging skill that pushed the limits of my abilities, I was able to see the differences as clear as day.

That's why, before sending you off to conquer the world with your newfound learning skills, I'd like to share a word of caution: your brain is a highly complex and finely tuned instrument, and you have just given it some serious upgrades. Like any finely tuned, high-performance instrument, insufficient maintenance can lead to poor performance, or worse, failure.

Many students discover this the same way that I did when they first begin SuperLearning. They're amazed at their ability to read faster and remember more but complain of excessive exhaustion, hunger, or an insatiable desire for naps. Remember: the brain consumes about 20 percent of our body's energy and resources. When you're operating it as rigorously as you now know how to, the added drain is palpable.

To combat this, there are a number of high-performance habits I would encourage you to consider.

First and foremost is sleep. While you may realize the importance of sleep, you probably don't give it nearly the respect or the priority it deserves. In the over 225 interviews I've done with some of the world's foremost superhumans, sleep is one of the few things that comes up time and time again. In a recent monthly challenge for my private mastermind community, sport sleep coach Nick Littlehales shed light on how broken the average person's sleep regimen really is.

When we sleep, our brains are hard at work, conducting a great number of processes that scientists have only begun to understand. Chief among these is the movement of memories from short-term to long-term memory and routine maintenance of our neurons and synapses. If, then, you neglect to sleep enough, your brain is incapable of creating or maintaining strong memories—plain and simple. Consider that the next time you choose to stay up late cramming for an exam or presentation.

What's more, research has proven that our brains can only clean up after themselves during sleep. When we use our brains intensively, metabolic waste builds up— just like it does in our muscles. In our brains, however, this waste causes those feelings of fogginess, pressure, and irritability that we all know too well. What most of us don't know is that our brains, unlike our muscles, are completely unable to clear this metabolic waste while we're awake.

Because of this, napping becomes a powerful tool for many SuperLearners. When I was studying intensively at INSEAD, I made a habit of napping nearly every single day. To this day, you'll often catch me dozing off in the middle of the day, especially on days that call for a lot of speed-reading or heavy-duty learning. Believe it or not, I'll often schedule in free time after something particularly challenging, such as a Russian lesson. Not only does a quick, twenty- to twenty-four-minute nap help clear metabolic waste, it restores alertness better than even the strongest cup of coffee. There are other benefits as well. Years ago, I had the opportunity to interview former Navy SEAL trainer turned sleep expert Dr. Kirk Parsley for my podcast. In the episode, we discussed the ways in which a properly-timed nap in the middle of an intensive learning period can condense the learning curve. According to Dr. Parsley, this is one of his secret strategies for integrating new knowledge quickly. For this reason, I've covered sleep extensively on my podcast. I encourage you to check out some of the episodes I've curated for you at http://jle.vi/bonus.

Proper rest periods aren't just about sleep, though. In fact, planning structured rest periods into your study sessions is yet another way to improve your focus and learning. One common method is called The Pomodoro Technique, named after the small tomato-shaped kitchen timers. In this method, you study or learn for twenty-five minutes, followed by a five-minute break. You then repeat this cycle four times, until it's time for a longer break. It sounds crazy, but it actually works. This is partly because taking periodic breaks allows us to rest, grab a drink of water, stand up, and get our blood circulating. This, in turn, restores our focus and prevents us from burning out. But another possible reason that breaks are so beneficial is what psychologists call the "Zeigarnik effect." This effect states that our brains can better remember and retain things that are unfinished or incomplete. The effect was first described by psychologist Bluma Zeigarnik. As the story goes, Zeigarnik's professor noticed that a waiter seemed to have an easier time remembering unpaid orders. After the order had been paid and closed out, the knowledge seemed to disappear. Fortunately, as she and her colleagues discovered, this has practical uses too. By leaving things "unfinished," even if temporarily, we can enhance our own memory of them. Studies have shown that students who suspend their learning to do something unrelated actually remember better than those who don't.[17]

---

17   Bluma Zeigarnik, "Das Behalten Erledigter und Unerledigter Handlungen," *Psychologische Forschung* 9, no. 1 (December 1927): 1-85, http://dx.doi.org/10.1007/BF02409755; Fred McKinney, "Studies in the Retention of Interrupted Learning Activities," *Journal of Comparative Psychology* 19, no. 2 (April 1935): 265-296, http://citeseerx.ist.psu.edu/viewdoc/download?doi=10.1.1.66.8781&rep=rep1&type=pdf.

In other words, don't deprive yourself of occasional study breaks—they are helping you remember!

Another one of the recurring themes among the top performers I've interviewed is nutrition. No surprises there! Students and readers love to ask what "nootropics" or "smart drugs" I'm currently using, without first asking how I am fueling my brain. On this, the research is quite clear. A diet low in carbohydrates, devoid of sugar, and rich in high quality, natural fats will make your brain sing. It'll trim your waistline too. Omega 3 fatty acids, such as those found in fish and chia seeds, are particularly great.

Wait. Isn't all fat bad for you?

No!

Over the last decade, research has proven that the nutritional advice of yesteryear had it all wrong. Our brains and bodies love to have a consistent source of energy. But this isn't possible when your blood sugar resembles a cutting-edge rollercoaster. Minimizing processed carbohydrates—particularly sugar—helps stabilize your blood glucose. What's more, on the extreme end of the spectrum, a high fat and low carb diet can put your body into a state of ketosis. This means that your body is burning fat as a source of fuel!

It sounds pretty good. It feels even better! Running on ketones is such a performance boost that many people choose to fast to get into this state. Some keep it simple at 18 hours, but others fast for a full 120! You should of course consult your doctor before swearing off food for a week. But at the very least, it's a good idea to switch out the starchy breakfast cereal for a few eggs and an avocado.

The third major theme for brain performance is also no surprise: exercise. I've seen so many students get into "panic" mode before an exam. They barely make time to eat—much less the "luxury" of working out. This is a huge mistake. When we exercise, we do much more than maintain the health of our bodies—the vessels that carry around and protect our brains. Exercise also has dramatic effects on our neurochemistry. Even a light workout can improve mood, lower stress, increase alertness, and enhance memory. In fact, some research has demonstrated that learning is easier while the body is in motion. So if you want to bring an audiobook with you on your bike ride, by all means. It won't hurt to invest in a standing desk while you're at it.

Once you've covered these three bases, everything else is in the realm of nitty-gritty details—and is quite honestly outside the scope of this book. It's the type of stuff we cover every single week on my podcast. Therefore, if you'd like to learn more about it, I suggest you visit us at http://superhumanacademy.com. Meditation, getting enough oxygen, and exposing yourself to bright, natural light during the day all help a great deal. Nootropics, ranging from green tea all the way up to modafinil are also quite useful and worth experimentation—with your doctor's approval. But none of these can help you if you neglect the three foundations upon which brain health is built: sleep, exercise, and nutrition.

It really is that simple, and it really is that important.

You may be the kind of person looking to squeeze out an additional 10 percent here and there. You might be curious about things like mushroom coffee (my current nootropic of choice), cold showers (another favorite), or neurofeedback training. By all means, experiment away! But first, make sure you have those three absolutely dialed in.

Look at it this way. If you've come this far, you've now invested a considerable amount of time and energy upgrading your brain. This is an upgrade that can and will change the way you live your life.

So please: protect your investment, and treat your brain right.

After all, it's one of the few organs that you can neither replace nor live without.

CONCLUSION

"Once you stop learning, you start dying."

—ALBERT EINSTEIN

When I began writing the first version of the Become a SuperLearner online course, I never could have imagined what it would become. Over the last five years, the creation of three courses, and the writing and publication of three books, we've touched the lives of hundreds of thousands of people. We've enabled them to finish graduate degrees, create dream jobs, start companies, and pick up fulfilling hobbies.

Along the way, by researching and teaching these powerful techniques, I have learned as much as my students, if not more. I've gone from being another victim of "information overload" to the unlikely champion of a movement to overcome it. And as I've taken up the mantle of this cause, my life has been given more meaning and purpose than I could've ever imagined.

The SuperLearner methodology is proof that we can unlock the hidden potential of our magnificent brains. It's proof that we can claim our birthright as exceptional learners and learn anything our heart desires.

In these pages, you have discovered the little-known techniques to do it all. You understand not only how your brain works but how to prime it for learning. You know the strategies to maintain its interest and use it the way evolution intended. You are now able to tap into the tremendous power of your visual memory using the same ancient memory techniques as world record holders. What's more, you have a framework for maintaining your memories long term. A framework that will save you countless hours no matter what you choose to learn.

But learning is far more than just memory and review. Fortunately, you also possess the skills to deconstruct any subject and create the perfect plan of attack. You know how to pre-read and analyze anything you wish to learn. And, with some practice, you're even poised to double or triple your reading speed, while retaining a high level of comprehension.

As you go on to learn the next subject that piques your

curiosity, you'll be astonished by the power of these seemingly simple skills. By leveraging brute force learning and cross-pollination, you'll not only learn more but do so with greater joy and engagement. By teaching others and developing fun ways to test your knowledge, you'll learn even the most complex subjects in record time. And while there are more advanced techniques to learn and expand upon, you now know far more than the 20 percent that yields 80 percent of the results.

In short, you will come to recognize yourself for what you truly are: a bona fide SuperLearner.

I truly believe that the lessons contained in the pages of this book are the most important skills I can bestow upon another human being. They are among the greatest gifts I have ever been given, and now, they are yours to use, enjoy, share, and improve upon.

ACKNOWLEDGMENTS

———

First, I'd like to thank my beautiful wife, Limmor, for giving me the support, strength, and the time to write this book at the expense of many other things. You are the greatest source of joy in my life. Thank you for listening to me think out loud, for being silly when I need it most, and for celebrating my wins even when I don't.

I also owe a great deal of credit to my loving parents, Lynn Ann and Meir. Had I been given the same challenges and any other parents, my life would never have turned out as blessed as it has. Thank you for teaching me to always march to the beat of my own drummer, instilling strong values in me, and never once doubting my potential. I am the man I am because of you.

To my incredibly supportive godparents and mentors, Linda and David. Thank you for always being the most vocal part of my fan club, for going above and beyond the job description, and for supporting me through the good times and the bad.

Of course, without the support of my team, I could never have written this book. To Allison, Armie, Brandon, Dimitris, Erick, Leslie, Malou, Monique, and Romina, thank you for believing in me and my mission and for all of your hard work to make our company what it is.

I also want to give a shout-out to our design and creative agency, the GoCrayons team. To Elaiza, Ron-Ron, Ronwell, and the entire staff—thank you for turning my ideas into beautiful realities.

Over the last seven years, I've had a number of mentors who taught me a great deal of what I share in this book, including Dr. Lev and Anna Goldentouch. The same is true of Dr. Anthony Metivier, who also taught me how to make an incredible living teaching it. Thank you for your generosity, friendship, and mentorship. I hate to think where I'd be without it.

On that note: a few teachers get a bad rap early on in this book, but the truth is, there were a number of deeply passionate and dedicated teachers who saw the potential in me despite it all. These include Mr. Scarola, Mrs. Carbone, Mr. Mount, Sharon Rodriguez, and Todd Dwyer, to name a few. Thank you for nurturing my curiosity and my intellect and showing me the power of the written word.

To Joe Polish and the entire Genius Network Team: thank you for challenging me to be the best entrepreneur I can and for surrounding me with the types of people who inspire me to do more.

And lastly, to the incredible team at Scribe, most notably Tucker, Hal, and Natalie. This is easily the highest quality book I could have ever written, and I owe that largely to you and your incredible guided author process.

SPECIAL INVITATION

Thank you so much for taking the time to read this book. I hope it positively impacts your life in ways you can't even imagine. If you are passionate about improving your reading, memory, and learning, I'd like to invite you to join our thriving community of over twenty thousand Super-Learners. There, you can share your progress, learn from others, and stay up to date on the latest new content. To join, please visit http://jle.vi/bonus.

ABOUT THE AUTHOR

—

JONATHAN LEVI is a serial entrepreneur, keynote speaker, podcaster, and bestselling author of the *Become a SuperLearner* book and online course series. After struggling for decades as a student and "slow learner," Jonathan discovered a powerful methodology for learning faster and remembering more. Since 2014, Jonathan has taught this methodology to over 220,000 people in 205 countries and territories. His award-winning podcast, SuperHuman Academy, has been downloaded over 3 million times. Jonathan has been featured in such media outlets as The Wall Street Journal, Inc., BusinessInsider, and LifeHacker UK. He lives in Tel Aviv, Israel, with his wife, Limmor. To learn more, visit http:// superhumanacademy.com.

BIBLIOGRAPHY

———

Alemi, Minoo, and Saman Ebadi. "The Effects of Pre-reading Activities on ESP Reading Comprehension." *Journal of Language Teaching and Research* 1, no. 5 (September 2010): 569–577. https://doi.org/10.4304/jltr.1.5.569-577.

Azizifara, Akbar, Soghra Roshania, Habib Gowharya, and Ali Jamalinesarib. "The Effect of Pre-reading Activities on the Reading Comprehension Performance of Ilami High School Students." *Procedia - Social and Behavioral Sciences* 192 (June 24, 2015): 188–194. https://doi.org/10.1016/j.sbspro.2015.06.027.

Clement, John. "Students' Preconceptions in Introductory Mechanics." *American Journal of Physics* 50, no. 1 (1982): 66. https://doi.org/10.1119/1.12989.

Drubach, Daniel. *The Brain Explained.* New Jersey: Prentice-Hall, 2000.

Fisher, Dennis F., and Wayne L. Shebilske. *Eye Movements in Reading.* Cambridge, MA: Academic Press, 1983. https://doi.org/10.1016/B978-0-12-583680-7.50014-X.

Franklin, Benjamin. *The Autobiography of Benjamin Franklin.* New York: PF Collier & Son Company, 1909. Kindle.

Hsu, Jeremy. "How Much Power Does The Human Brain Require To Operate?" *Popular Science*, November 7, 2009. https://www.popsci.com/technology/article/2009-11/neuron-computer-chips-could-overcome-power-limitations-digital.

Isaacson, Walter. *Benjamin Franklin: An American Life*. New York: Simon & Schuster, 2003. Kindle.

Karpickea, Jeffrey D., and Henry L. Roediger III. "The Critical Importance of Retrieval for Learning." *Science* 319, no. 5865 (February 15, 2008): 966–968. http://dx.doi.org/10.1126/science.1152408.

Karpickea, Jeffrey D., and Janell R. Blunt. "Retrieval Practice Produces More Learning than Elaborative Studying with Concept Mapping." *Science* 331, no. 6018 (February 11, 2011): 772–775. http://dx.doi.org/10.1126/science.1199327.

Marinaccio, Jessica. "The Most Effective Pre-reading Strategies for Comprehension." Master's thesis, St. John Fisher College, 2012.

McClusky, H. Y. "An Experiment on the Influence of Preliminary Skimming on Reading." *Journal of Educational Psychology* 25, no. 7 (Oct 1934): 521–529. http://dx.doi.org/10.1037/h0070829.

McKinney, Fred. "Studies in the Retention of Interrupted Learning Activities." *Journal of Comparative Psychology* 19, no. 2 (April 1935): 265–296. http://citeseerx.ist.psu.edu/viewdoc/download?doi=10.1.1.66.8781&rep=rep1&type=pdf

Ong, Walter J. *Orality and Literacy*. Abingdon, UK: Routledge, 2002.

Rayner, Keith, Elizabeth R. Schotter, Michael E. J. Masson, Mary C. Potter, and Rebecca Treiman. "So Much to Read, So Little Time: How Do We Read, and Can Speed Reading Help?" *Psychological Science in the Public Interest* 17, no. 1 (January 14, 2016): 4–34. https://doi.org/10.1177/1529100615623267.

Rayner, Keith, Sarah J. White, Rebecca L. Johnson, and Simon P. Liversedge. "Raeding Wrods With Jubmled Lettres: There Is a Cost." *Psychological Science* 17, no. 3 (March 1, 2006): 192–193. http://dx.doi.org/10.1111/j.1467-9280.2006.01684.x.

Vázquez-García, Mario. "Collaborative-Group Testing Improves Learning and Knowledge Retention of Human Physiology Topics in Second-Year Medical Students." *Advances in Physiology Education* 42, no. 2 (June 1, 2018): 232–239. http://dx.doi.org/10.1152/advan.00113.2017.

Wagatsuma, Akiko, Teruhiro Okuyama, Chen Sun, Lillian M. Smith, Kuniya Abe, and Susumu Tonegawa. "Locus Coeruleus Input to Hippocampal CA3 Drives Single-Trial Learning of a Novel Context." *Proceedings of the National Academy of Sciences of the United States of America* January 9, 2018 115 (2) E310-E316. https://doi.org/10.1073/pnas.1714082115.

Zeigarnik, Bluma. "Das Behalten Erledigter und Unerledigter Handlungen." *Psychologische Forschung* 9, no. 1 (December 1927): 1–85. http://dx.doi.org/10.1007/BF02409755.